Lindsay G Thompson

History of the Fisheries of New South Wales

With a sketch of the laws by which they have been regulated

Lindsay G Thompson

History of the Fisheries of New South Wales
With a sketch of the laws by which they have been regulated

ISBN/EAN: 9783337329051

Printed in Europe, USA, Canada, Australia, Japan

Cover: Foto ©ninafisch / pixelio.de

More available books at **www.hansebooks.com**

blished by Authority of the New South Wales Commissioners for the World's Columbian Exposition, Chicago, 1893.

ISTORY OF THE FISHERIES

OF

NEW SOUTH WALES;

WITH

SKETCH OF THE LAWS BY WHICH THEY HAVE BEEN REGULATED:

BY

LINDSAY G. THOMPSON,
CHIEF INSPECTOR OF NEW SOUTH WALES FISHERIES.

)MPILED FROM OFFICIAL AND OTHER AUTHENTIC SOURCES.

Sydney:
CHARLES POTTER, GOVERNMENT PRINTER, PHILLIP-STREET.
1893.
[1s. 6d.]

CONTENTS.

CHAPTER I.

The Marine Fishing-grounds—Trawling—Fish-preserving Companies—The Herring Fishery 1–16

CHAPTER II.

Inland Waters Fisheries—Fish Acclimatisation—Marine and Fresh-water Pisciculture 17–26

CHAPTER III.

The Fisheries Laws and their Administration ... 26–43

CHAPTER IV.

The Fish Markets and the Fish Trade ... 44–51

CHAPTER V.

The Oyster Fisheries and the law governing them ... 52–72

CHAPTER VI.

Crustacea ... 73–75

CHAPTER VII.

The Whale Fisheries ... 76–88

CHAPTER VIII.

The Pearl-shell Fisheries ... 89–94

CHAPTER IX.

The Aboriginal Fisheries and Canoes and Fishing... 95–101

APPENDICES ... 102–126

PLATES AND MAPS.

The Fisheries of New South Wales.

CHAPTER I.

THE Fisheries of New South Wales have ever engaged more or less of public attention, for it had always been evident that, possessing a coast-line of such a contour as that which shapes the eastern boundary of the Colony, the possibilities of fish production must be enormous, and quite worth all the consideration which could be bestowed upon them.

The purpose of this pamphlet is to trace the history of the attempts made to utilise these fisheries, to review the laws by which, from period to period, they have been governed, and to offer such further information respecting them as the writer himself possesses, and official and other authentic records will supply.

It is hoped that a perusal of these pages will help to convey some idea of the extent and value of our piscine resources, and the so-far latent wealth which await only the aid of capital and enterprise to develop.

With such objects in view, it will be proper, in the first place, to attempt a brief description of—

THE MARINE FISHING-GROUNDS.

The marine fishing-grounds so far known to us extend along the entire length of the sea-board—some 700 miles. This sea-board, both in its inlets and its offing, is in a marked degree favourable to the development of the very large supply of food-fishes which inhabit it. It is indented by innumerable inlets and arms of the sea. It possesses many rivers whose embouchures are of large expanse. Its lakes and some of its bays and harbours are of vast extent, and its submarine conditions generally are of a character eminently adapted both as nursery and feeding grounds for fish. The following outline is intended to afford an idea of the position of these inlets with reference to Sydney, their naturally large resources, and their number and variety.

The fisheries are distributed into three large sections—the Northern, the Southern, and the Home divisions. The principal of these is the latter. It is shown on the map, and comprises all the tidal waters between Port Stephens and Bherrewerre, St. George's Basin. The metropolitan market is within easy reach from almost any point within this division, hence its value and its designation.

THE HOME DIVISION OF FISHERIES.

Port Stephens, about 90 miles to the northward of Sydney, takes a premier position amongst the fishing-stations—connected with a vast series of lakes (the Myall Lakes) with the Karuah River, Telligherry Creek, a dozen of important affluents, and miles upon miles of beaches and flats, suitable for seine-hauling, this immense water, some two or three times the size of Port Jackson, is, it may readily be conceived, one of the large factors in the metropolitan supply. At present it is out of reach of railway communication. This disadvantage may possibly be removed in the near future; but its produce is even now very readily conveyed by sea to Newcastle, and thence to Sydney by rapid steam or rail transit.

Hunter River.—The reaches on the lower part of this river are of more importance to Sydney as a prawn fishery than in the supply of line or net fish which they afford. Even the population of Newcastle is not adequately supplied by the Hunter. Most probably the great and constant destruction of immature fish by prawn-nets, an evil which legislation, though specially instituted in that direction, has so far failed to overcome, is responsible for this.

**Lake Macquarie.*—Since the opening of the North Coast Railway to Newcastle, this magnificent lake has become the most productive of our fisheries. Prior to that event it was valued only as a vast nursing and feeding ground. Owing to the difficulty of communication with Sydney, it found but little favour with the fishermen, the few who happened to be stationed there preferring to fish for the Chinese curers

---

* *See* Map—Appendices.

rather than risk the chance of landing their catch in good condition at the metropolitan market. The lake entrance being very shallow could be availed of only at certain states of the tide, and as the plan, which had been attempted, of sending the catch by boat to a steamer off the bar was found to be unsatisfactory, the only other available route was *via* Newcastle. This route involved a journey of some twelve miles over a very rough road, the transference of the fish to the steamboat, and at the Sydney end from the steamboat by cart to the fish-market. The result of all this handling and shaking, especially in the summer months, was, as might be expected, that a large proportion of the consignments were, on arrival at the market, unfit for human food.

All this difficulty is now of the past, the Chinamen have for the most part disappeared and European fishermen have taken their places. These latter have taxed the resources of the lake to what might be supposed their extreme limits, yet year after year it is found at the top of the list, both in the quantity and the quality of its yield.

This water, the largest in the lake system which occurs between Newcastle and Sydney, is of great expanse, it is nearly twenty miles in length, with an average width of four miles, and its contour is so broken by deeply-indented bays and recesses as to give a perimeter of about 300 miles. As with but comparatively small exception the whole extent of the shores are suitable for seine-hauling, it will be readily conceived that it offers unparalleled advantages to the professional fisherman.

Tuggerah Beach Lakes.—South from Lake Macquarie, and separated from it by a flat strip of land about a mile in width, begin the series of lakes known as Tuggerah, they are three in number, Manmurra, Budgewoi, and Tuggerah proper, they are all connected, and together have an extreme length from north to south of fourteen miles. Tuggerah is the largest, and the principal of the series, it has communication with the sea at a small rocky opening in the beach about seven miles north from a well-known boat harbour called Terrigal. The entrance is very broken and shallow, and is rarely available, even for open boats; still, however, during the prevalence of westerly winds which blow off the coast fishermen occasionally navigate it. Now, however, these waters, which, like Lake Macquarie, abound in flats, shallows, and long foreshores, and are fish-producing to an enormous extent, are tapped by the North Coast Railway at Wyong. The railway station is reached by a creek of that name, about four miles in length, situated about north-west from the sea entrance. Fish are conveyed from these lakes to Sydney by rail in about two hours and a half.

Broken Bay, the Hawkesbury, Pitt Water, and Brisbane Water.—South from Tuggerah and situated considerably nearer to Port Jackson is Broken Bay, the embouchure of the far-famed Hawkesbury River, with its extensive arms, Brisbane Water on the north and Pitt Water on the south. These waters, from their ready accessibility and fish-producing capabilities, have always ranked, and still rank, amongst the most important of our fishing-grounds. The beaches bounding these waters present the most favourable conditions to net fishermen, and the upper reaches of the river and the mud flats of its various tributaries comprising Mullet, Mooney, Marra-Marra, Berowra, and Mangrove Creeks, have helped to supply Sydney for many years past, and still continue to do so. The North Coast Railway now taps this river at a point locally known as the Flat Rock, and by its means the produce of its more upper waters is conveyed to the metropolis with the greatest facility, and with but little loss even in the height of summer.

Port Jackson and Parramatta River.—On the shores of Port Jackson stands Sydney, the metropolis of New South Wales. It is the centre of the Home Division of Fisheries, and the point to which all fish produce converges. At one time Port Jackson held a premier position amongst the fishing-grounds for all kinds of the best net-fish, but it has lost much of its value. This is owing not only to the pollution of its waters by the sewage of a large city and constant disturbance by the traffic of innumerable craft, but to a wanton destructive process of netting to which every bay and flat have been subjected. Legislation, to which I shall refer to later on, has done something towards counteracting this evil, and possibly when the scheme for carrying the sewage direct to the ocean shall have been sufficiently long in operation to allow of the feeding-grounds recovering themselves, the metropolitan harbour may again in some degree yield its original supply. To the north of Port Jackson, between Manly and Pitt Water, are a series of small lagoons, Curl-Curl, Deewhy and Narrabeen. These lagoons are most

---

* *See* Map—Appendices.

valuable breeding-grounds and nurseries for many kinds of edible fish, and care is taken to prevent them from being ravaged by the operation of netters.

Botany Bay and George's River.—Some 10 miles south from Port Jackson lies Botany Bay and its valuable tributaries the George's and Woronora Rivers—these are amongst the most prolific of our grounds, and are esteemed of high value, not only on account of the enormous supply they so continuously yield, but by reason of their proximity to Sydney and its southern suburbs, and the many ready means which exist for the transit of fish. Fish can be sent by train, by tram, and by several lines of road from these waters, which are of value not only to the professional fisherman but to quite an army of amateur line fishermen also. It is not at all unusual on holidays, and on Saturdays and Sundays, for some 300 boats to be engaged here in line-fishing, each boat having from three to six occupants.

Port Hacking.—South from Botany, and about 6 miles distant, is Port Hacking. It is a splendid fishing-ground, but as bordering on the National Park it has been considered proper to restrict its use for purposes of public recreation and amusement. Netting in any part of it is prohibited by special Act of Parliament, and the rights of public thus created as against the net fishermen are most zealously guarded.

**Lake Illawarra.*—Between Port Hacking and this lake a stretch of 33 miles of rock-bound coast occurs with nothing to break it except an artificially-formed harbour basin at Wollongong. Some 4 miles south from Wollongong is Lake Illawarra; this water bears on the south somewhat of the relation to Sydney which Lake Macquarie does on the north, being an important breeding-ground and nursery and a factor in the fish supply; moreover, nearly the whole line of its shores is comprised of flats and shallows, and seines can be used in almost any part of it. It has but a narrow and indifferent entrance to the sea which, except in very calm weather, cannot be used even by fishing-boats; it is tapped at several points by the South Coast Railway, and by this mode of transit its produce is despatched.

Shoalhaven and Crookhaven Rivers.—Passing southerly from Lake Illawarra along another considerable stretch of

---
* See Map—Appendices.

unindented rock-bound coast the Shoalhaven and Crookhaven Rivers are reached. These rivers are navigable by coastal steamboats for some distance; they abound with fish of all kinds common to our other waters, but their comparative remoteness from Sydney has hitherto militated against the transmission of their produce to market except during the winter months; the steamboat service is not available for the work, as between Shoalhaven and Port Jackson are several ports of call, so that the time of arrival at the terminal point cannot always be calculated. The difficulty in the way of fully utilising this prolific fishery will, however, soon be of the past. An extension of the South Coast Railway to Jervis Bay has been projected, and the line is now in process of construction to an intermediate point, the village of Nowra, a settlement on the Shoalhaven River, about 10 miles from the sea; on completion of this extension this fishery will be placed within a very few hours distance from Sydney. Just immediately south of the Crookhaven River is a lagoon known as Lake Wolumla; it is about 3½ miles long by 1 mile in width; it is a natural breeding and feeding ground, and its adaptability for the propagation of marine fish by artificial means cannot be too strongly asserted.

Bherrewerre or Saint George's Basin.—This water forms the southern limit of the Home Fisheries Division; equally with other waters it contains fish in abundance, and good hauling-grounds exist along nearly the whole length of its shores. But its remoteness from the metropolis and the difficulty of transporting the fish which would have to be carted for 20 miles over a rough bush road to the nearest steamboat wharf precludes its present use as a fishing-station. On completion of the extension of the South Coast Railway to Jervis Bay— the basin will be brought within 2 miles of train haulage, and its produce will largely enhance the fish supply. Jervis Bay, a very large stretch of water to the north-east of St. George's Basin, is similarly situated; its immense resources must remain locked up until suitable modes of transit are established.

THE NORTHERN AND SOUTHERN DIVISIONS OF FISHERIES.

These embrace respectively the line of coast from Port Stephens northerly to the Tweed River, and from Saint George's Basin southerly to Cape Howe; they include many navigable rivers, and extensive lakes, and lagoons, but

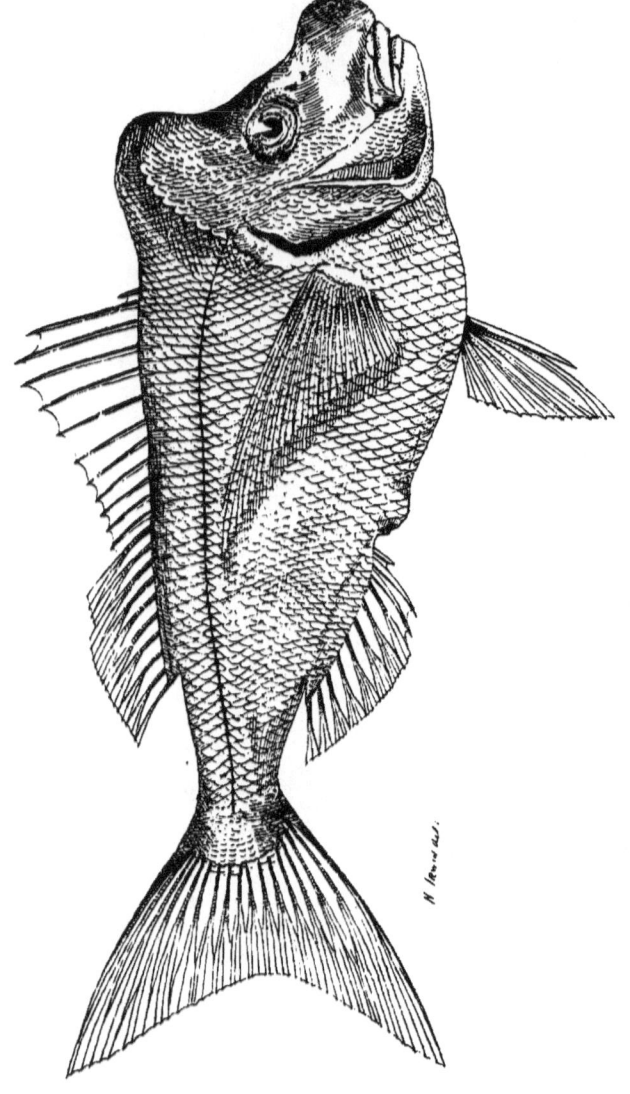

SCHNAPPER. *Pagrus unicolor.*

Attains a weight of 35 lbs

as fishing-grounds they are, for the most part, practically untouched, and so far as the home divisional fisherman is concerned are almost unknown; yet their producing capabilities are not to be ranked as at all inferior to the grounds in the Home Division; they abound with fish of all the species common to our coast, and if the smallest reliance is to be placed upon the reports of the Fisheries Inspectors and Pilots or Custom Officers stationed at the mouths of the various inlets of such rivers as the Tweed, the Richmond, the Clarence, the Bellinger, the Nambuccra, the Macleay, the Manning, the Clyde, the Moruya, Twofold Bay, and other waters of less importance, there cannot be a doubt that a profitable industry lies ready for immediate development when the necessary enterprise and capital are forthcoming.

A reference to the map will show the large extent to which the whole coast-line from north to south is broken by rivers, creeks, lakes, bays, and other inlets, each of them abounds with fish; their existence alone is ample warrant for asserting the unusual advantages which New South Wales possess for establishing an enormous export trade in fish. But really her advantages only begin here. She has besides untold wealth to acquire when she places under contribution the vast stores held in trust by the deep sea itself; these untold stores it is now proposed to consider under the title of

THE OFFING FISHERIES.

These exist along the whole length of the coast-line and wide-off for a distance of 10 miles or more in water at a depth from about 30 to 50 fathoms; the position of some of these in the more immediate vicinity of Port Jackson and the metropolitan market, it is proposed presently to define. The schnapper, which, for economic purposes, may be ranked with the cod of the northern hemisphere, is distributed with remarkable regularity over all of these grounds—whatever the formation of the coast may be, this fish, perhaps the most valuable, and the most abundant of all our forms is never absent, and being essentially a rock fish in its habits is not migratory. The same may be said of its congener the bream, and in a lesser degree of the flathead, whiting, blackfish, tailer, tarwhine, garfish, and other varieties which frequent as well the bays and estuaries of our harbours and lakes.

There are most important schnapper-grounds existing at varying distances from all the main headlands between the South Head of Broken Bay and the North Head of Port Jackson; there are, at least, a score of school of fish-grounds within these limits. Vast quantities of fish have been taken in every one of them, especially along the line of submerged rocks known as Long Reef, which can be traced for a distance of five miles off shore, and on the wide off grounds off Narrabeen Bight. Bumboras or sunken rocks are found in this bight, and they, like all others on the coast are the favourite resort of the schnapper fishermen during particular conditions of the currents. It is said that schnapper have been taken in large quantities about ten miles wide off from Long Reef in about 35 to 40 fathoms of water. Excepting those off Deewhy there are no recognised grounds between Long Reef and the North Head of Port Jackson. Off this head is a line of reefs jutting out under water which, like those at Long Reef, forms a series of schnapper grounds, which had once a splendid reputation, but are now not much to be depended upon; possibly these, like the grounds about three miles due east from Port Jackson have suffered deterioration from the constant discharge from the mud-punts of silt and harbour refuse. Continuing southerly, the next grounds resorted to by fishermen are off the Flagstaff and Mud Island; the next of importance are at varying distances from the rocky islet off Coogee Bay. These are favourite grounds for the various fishing clubs which pursue their recreation in small steam vessels, and from force of numbers and the ease with which they can shift from one spot to another are able to count out more fish for a fair day's outing than any of the professional fishing crews. About fourteen miles eastward of these Coogee grounds a shell-bank was discovered by Mr. James M'Carthy, an amateur fisherman—it carries only about 20 to 30 fathoms of water; but it is so narrow that vessels find great difficulty in lying-to on it; the ridge extends in a north-west to south-east direction for about a mile, and the soundings in the immediate neighbourhood show 70 to 90 fathoms. Another, the Jerusalem Bank, about fifty miles east-northerly from Wollongong, carrying 20 fathoms of water, was found in 1876 by Captain Largie of the barque "Jerusalem." It was searched for subsequently by Captain Hixson, the President of the Marine Board, but without success. So far as is known the search has not been repeated. Then there is a bank about three miles east by north from Bowen Island, off the mouth of Jervis Bay, carrying 30 to 35 fathoms of water. Another bank exists ten miles east by north from Wollongong carrying 30 fathoms, and one five miles east from Kiama carrying 40 fathoms. Besides, there are the Sir John Young's banks, about three to four miles off the south headland of the Shoalhaven Bight—these consist of an inner and an outer bank of rock formation, they carry a depth of 7 to 12 fathoms of water; the water around the banks dips to 20 and 40 fathoms. The banks are not much used by fishermen. In calm weather they are easily recognisable by the rip of the current. The accidental discovery of these banks suggests that in the conformation of the ocean bottom they may be found to occur in numbers, and be fish-bearing to such a degree as to give quite distinctive features to the fisheries of the future.

Between Coogee and Cape Banks, the northern headland of Botany Bay, the fishing grounds are wholly confined to those in the offing; there are about a dozen schnapper grounds within these limits, but none of them of much importance. Excepting the long line of rocky ground which forms the submarine extension of Cape Banks, none hereabout possess the necessary conditions for school fish; as is the case on all foul grounds fish roam about from patch to patch in small schools. The entrance to Botany Bay is foul as a rule, and although wide of Cape Banks there are some very fair school-fish grounds, yet they have never been appreciated by fishermen, who prefer the Bumboras and off-shore grounds to the southward of Cape Solander, Longnose, and Curranulla Head, notwithstanding the strength of the southerly current which, off some of these headlands, runs in the summer months like a sluice.

Mr. Alexander Oliver, M.A., now the President of the Land Appeal Court, at one time a Commissioner of Fisheries for this Colony, and who as a recognised authority has given very frequent and valuable contributions to our fisheries literature, thus describes in an interesting paper on the fisheries, the grounds from *Botany to Wattamolle*:—

"At and off the entrance of Botany and Curranulla Head there are several well known schnapper grounds, about 2 miles within Curranulla Bight (the "Bate Bay" of our charts) is a famous ground known to fishermen as the Mary, Merry, or Shamrock Rock, for it goes under all these names. It is a sunken flat rock, or series of rocks, with about 8 to 11 fathoms of water, situated at the point of a reef which runs from a little boat-harbour called 'Doughboy,' about ½ a mile to southward. Tons upon tons of schnappers have been taken off this ground, which however is difficult for a stranger to find, as the cross-bearing marks are not easily described. The whole of this Port Hacking or Curranulla Bight is one vast nursery and feeding-ground for fish, and the harbour and river of Port Hacking at its southern extremity is second only to Broken Bay as a net ground. Here are caught generally the first gar-fish and mullet of the season, both which fish come to us from the southward, generally seeking the smooth harbour waters after a heavy south and south-easterly weather, and, after a few days continuing their progress northward, and putting in at every inlet or river-mouth lying in their course. A cable-length or so distant from 'Jibben Head,' the southern point of the entrance to Port Hacking, lies Jibben 'bumbora,' a fishing-mark of great repute, but not now much resorted to for school-fish, *i.e.*, the schnapper of about 4 to 6 or 7 years old, and found on the off-shore grounds in large schools, as distinguished from the native, which is the same fish at a latter stage of growth, but frequenting different haunts (the shoals off headlands, sunken rocks, and river-points). Passing south, the inshore grounds off Marly Head and Wattamolle are next reached, and this latter point forms the Sydney and Botany fisherman's *Ultima Thule*. Indeed, these southern fishing-grounds are rarely troubled, except in the winter months, when the wind generally blows off the shore, and is fair for both the up and down trip."

This description of the value of the offing grounds in the immediate vicinity of Port Jackson may be applied with equal correctness to the offing of the whole coast-line. Schnapper and other fish can be captured in quantity at almost any point. To give an instance, the harbour and river entrances are more or less bar-bound, and steam-boats trading to them have sometimes to await a favouring tide to run in. While waiting it is usual for the passengers to pass the time in fishing, and quite considerable quantities of fish are frequently taken in this way. It will thus be evident that the offing in its length and breadth is one vast fishing-ground, wonderfully prolific, and as yet practically unworked.

TRAWLING.

But it is not to the line fisherman only that this extensive ground can be made to yield its wealth; at frequent intervals along the coast-line occur extensive bights, having so far as is known firm bottoms, clear of impediments, over which the beam trawl could be drawn for miles; such as these exist between Newcastle and Port Stephens, off Tuggerah, off Shoalhaven, and off numerous other points; on each fish abound. Some two years since a vessel derelict was discovered drifting in the course of passing ships off the Port Stephens Bight; she was recovered and towed towards the land and

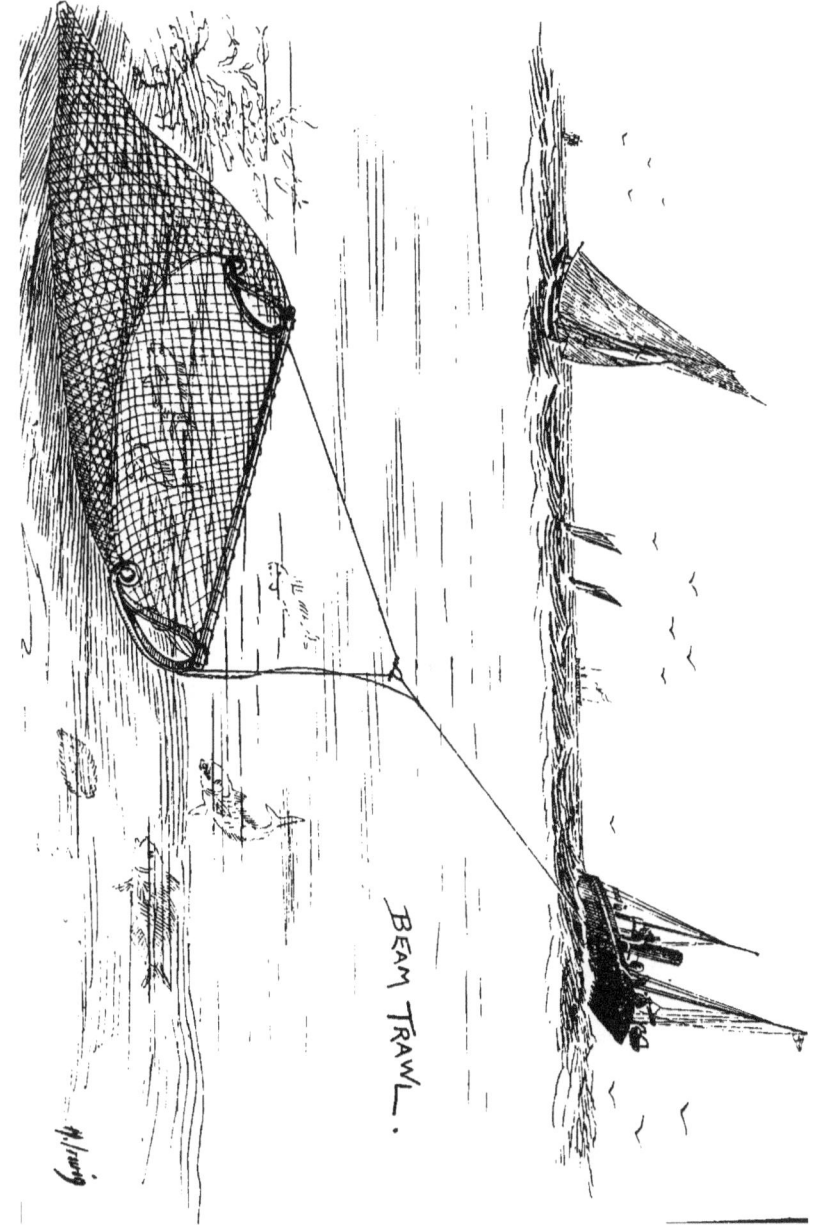

sunk at some distance from it; being still a danger to craft trading along that coast it was resolved to destroy her by dynamite. A consequence of the explosion was to throw up whiting, flathead, flounders, and other fish to the surface of the water in enormous quantities; it may readily be inferred that the systematic trawling of these bights would yield most satisfactory results.

In this Colony there are not any vessels having facilities for working the trawl-net. On one occasion rough trawling gear was improvised on a small steam tug. The trial was intended to occupy a week, but as regards the amount of work done the results were disappointing, this was due entirely to the severity of the weather and the unfitness of the steamer to contend against a heavy sea. The trawl could be put over the side only twice during the trip and then only for a few hours, so that the actual length of ground traversed was very short. On the first occasion the trawl was lowered about 6 miles off the south head of Botany Bay in 40 fathoms of water; it was kept down three hours when it was hauled in from 55 fathoms down. The trawl showed evidence of having been well on the ground, and its contents were three dozen Lepidotrigla, several John Dorey (Zeus Australis), two dozen stingrays, four dozen skates (Rai), several saw-fish.

The trawl was again lowered four miles off Curranulla Reef in 22 fathoms of water and drawn in a south-easterly direction for three hours when it was raised in 40 fathoms of water. The haul consisted of several dozen of Lepidotrigla, fourteen John Dorey, a number of stingrays, a flathead, three small soles.

Looked upon as a whole the results of this experiment, carried out under such extremely unfavourable conditions, were regarded in scientific quarters as decidedly promising—the existence of a true skate was thought to be a valuable discovery and the abundance of the John Dorey as also important, for it was hitherto considered very rare, while its quality as a food-fish is unrivalled in the world. But whether regarded commercially as successful or unsuccessful, this attempt at deep water trawling in New South Wales proves incontestably that we know very little of the inhabitants of our ocean floor; indeed, of the few fish dredged up, the Lepidotrigla and Rai were of a species utterly unknown, and others were extremely rare. We do know, however, that ground fish of various species exist in abundance, and this alone should be sufficient warrant for anticipating successful results from a trawling expedition properly manned and equipped and assisted with favourable weather.

Of course it is scarcely reasonable to expect that private enterprise will step in and prosecute this industry on the basis of little more than the bare assumption of ultimate success. But under proper representation the Government would, doubtless, direct the institution of a trawl-survey to test the suitability of some of the large bights already named.

This, while it would be more expeditious and far less expensive than a hydrographic survey, would supply just the information it will most concern the intending trawler to possess; as, for instance, not only the depths of water and character of bottom but the fish producing capabilities as well; while to the public it would evidence the probable value of fish capture by trawling as items of national economy and wealth.

The equipment necessary for a trawl-survey would be a small steamboat sufficiently fitted and manned by an ordinary crew, but supplemented by one or two expert certificated trawl fishermen;—of these several are to be found amongst the employés in the Marine Departments of the Crown.

In concluding this brief description of the fishing-grounds of New South Wales it may be fitting, perhaps, to remark that we have in our seas a wonderful variety of fishes not surpassed in numbers or excellence in any country in the world. We have herrings of various kinds annually skirting our coast in countless shoals, we have shoals of mackerel, tailer, king-fish, trevally, and yellow-tail, gar-fish, whiting, schnapper, mullet, &c. Of the mullet (*mugil grandis*), which, under proper system and treatment, might be made of immense value to the country, it is hardly possible to write in language too extravagant. It is of all our fishes the one that offers the greatest inducement for a special fishery. It makes its appearance in very large shoals during the months of April and May, travelling in a northerly direction, and showing a disposition to enter every inlet and harbour along its course. It is at that time in the finest condition and full of roe, and is prosecuting its migration simply in search of suitable spawning-grounds;—the quantity which could be consumed in a fresh state during this special season which lasts only about six or eight weeks would be very small in proportion to the quantity which could be captured, and it would be quite practicable to utilise the vast numbers of this splendid

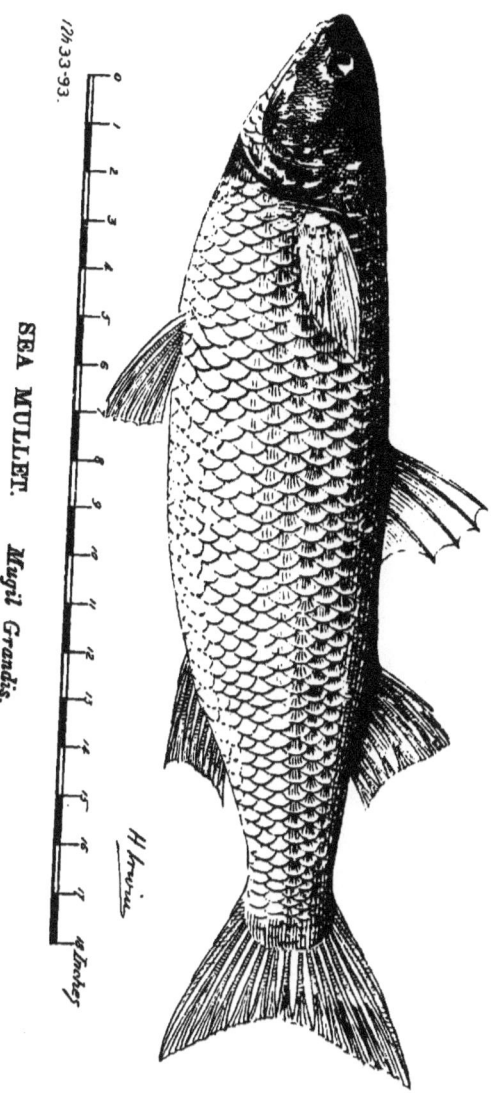

SEA MULLET. *Mugil Grandis.*

fish by preservation in a marketable form for home consumption, or export. It is not unusual to salt and smoke the mullet, but its very fatness makes it a bad fish for this mode of treatment—it takes salt too readily and is apt to become rancid. The roe, however, salted and smoked is equal to anything of the kind so prepared, and in that state it is rapidly bought up in quantity.

With a fish of such richness, delicacy, and distinctive flavour it was supposed that no plan of preservation has been found to surpass that generally adopted for the salmon (a fish possessing many of its qualities), viz., boiling and hermetically sealing in tin cans. This process has been adopted on several occasions, and always with success. Mullet thus preserved was displayed at the great International Fisheries Exhibition, London, 1883, at the Colonial and Indian Exhibition, 1888, and at the several exhibitions held in one or other of the Australian Colonies, and always received the highest commendation, not only from the public but also from official experts.

As the outcome of these experiments made by the Fisheries Commissioners, two companies, one at Cape Hawke and another at the Clarence River, have embarked in this industry with every probability of immediate success. Possessing, as New South Wales does, the raw material in such unlimited abundance, it is difficult to forecast the ultimate results of these small beginnings.

THE CAPE HAWKE FISH-PRESERVING COMPANY.

The works are situated on Wallis Lake, about a mile from its entrance;—though not extensive, they are capable of turning out about 600 tins per diem—indeed, the establishment of the factory in the first instance was purely speculative, and at the start the venture was met with the great difficulty of having to contend against the imported article, which has a strong hold upon the public taste; however, owing to the excellence of their arrangements, and the undoubted value of some species of our fish for preserving purposes, the proprietors have been rewarded by a ready sale for their productions; so much so indeed, that the orders during the last Lenten season exceeded the quantity which the manufactory was able to turn out.

The Company, so far, has confined its operations to the canning of smoked fish, in a style similar to that employed for kippered herrings and Findon haddocks. It is found that our whiting, bream, and mullet are most suitable for this process, and these species can be captured in large quantities. It is the intention shortly to attempt the canning of cray-fish;—some samples of this crustacean have indeed already been put up as an experiment, and it is claimed that they are far superior to the imported canned lobster. As the supply of this cray-fish is during five months of the year practically inexhaustible, there seems every prospect of a large trade being opened up. The Company proposes to display its wares at the forthcoming World's Columbian Exposition, Chicago, 1893, and a favourable report from competent judges is hoped for.

THE CLARENCE RIVER FRESH FISH AND CANNING COMPANY (LIMITED)

more fully described in the Appendices, is a registered Company, possessing a fairly sufficient capital—the works are at Iluka, at the entrance to the Clarence River—the aim of the Company is to establish a trade in the supply of fresh fish to the metropolitan markets by the aid of steam traders, fitted with proper appliances to maintain the requisite temperature. In addition, as its title implies, it has embarked in the business of canning fish for export, and, like its sister establishment at Cape Hawke, bids fair to secure remunerative results. An exhibit from this Company also will be on view at the approaching Columbian Exposition.

THE HERRING FISHERIES.

The herring fisheries on the New South Wales coast have not so far received the attention which their importance demands; indeed this fish is so very rarely seen in the Sydney fish market as to warrant the belief that the Australian seas are barren of this species which form such a large source of wealth in other countries. The late Sir William Macleay, a principal authority on all questions connected with fish and fisheries, says, in a paper read before the Linnean Society, that the very reverse is the fact. There is no sea on the globe favoured with a more rich or varied supply of fishes of the herring tribe than that which washes our shores. That they are seldom seen is due to the fact that the shoals do not as a rule enter the harbours on the coast, and that to fish for

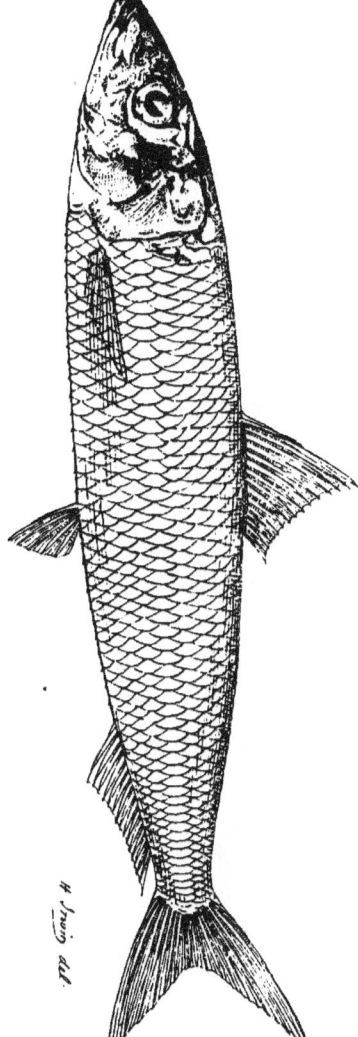

MARAY. *Clupea sagax.*

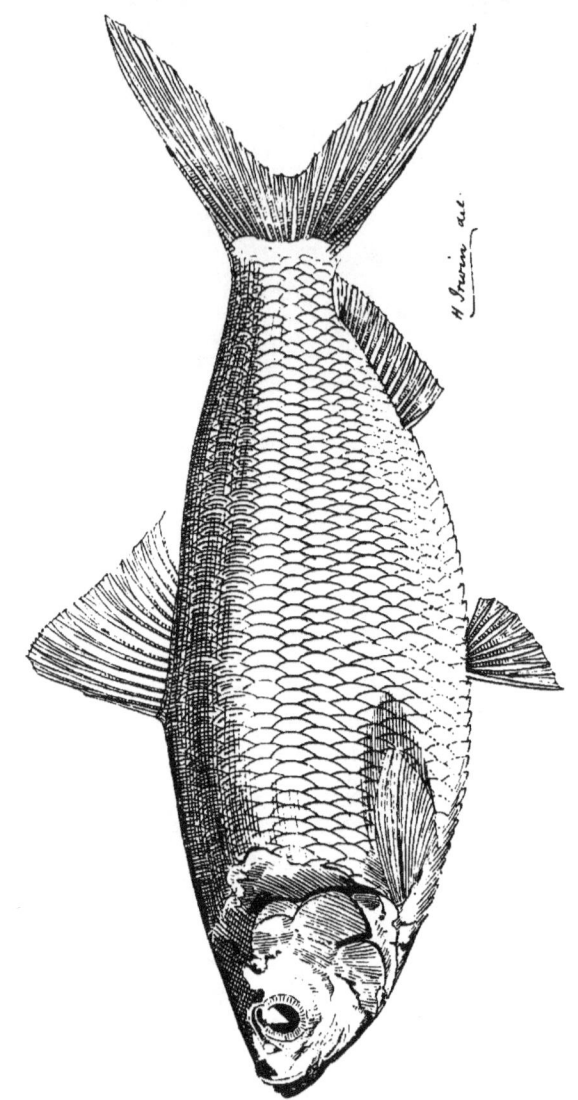

THE SOUTHERN HERRING.   *Clupea Sundiaca.*

them in the open sea would require appliances not at present in the possession of our fishermen. These species, as might be expected, are different from those of the Northern Hemisphere, but in excellence as edibles certainly not inferior.

A species of herring (*clupea sagax*) almost identical with the English pilchard makes its appearance on the coast of New South Wales annually in June or July. It is called by the fishermen *Maray*, probably a native name, though this term is sometimes applied to other species of herring. The shoals are described as enormous, covering miles of sea and accompanied by flights of birds and numbers of large fishes. These shoals are generally observed from 1 to 3 miles from the land, and are always proceeding in a northerly direction. The same fish is reported by Dr. Hector, F.R.S., Director of the Colonial Museum, Wellington, New Zealand, to visit the East Coast of Otago every year in February or March. In 1877 " a shoal was observed there migrating southwards. It extended as far as the eye could reach, followed by multitudes of gulls, mutton-birds, barracoota, and porpoises. So densely packed were they that by dipping a pitcher into the sea it would be drawn out half full of fish; so that by the use of large boats and suitable nets thousands of tons could have been caught." There is much that is curious about the migrations of this fish: all the shoals which pass here in winter are going north, while the shoals visiting Otago in summer are going south. It is a matter for inquiry— " Are they the same fishes returning to their homes in the Antarctic seas after months of travel in search of spawning grounds? If so, how far north do they go? And where are their breeding grounds?"

A species of herring common on the New South Wales coast, is the *clupea sundiaca*. " This species can be readily distinguished from the *sagax* by its much deeper and more compressed body, and the bright golden band on each side near the back." Shoals of this fish sometimes visit Port Jackson. Sir William Macleay relates that on one morning he found the beach at Elizabeth Bay strewed with bushels of them, left by a fisherman who had hauled his seine there during the night and taken away as many as he could. Like the Maray (*sagax*) it visits our coasts in winter in enormous shoals. It seems probable that its breeding grounds are not far distant, as it is to be found in the Hawkesbury, about Mullet Island, at all seasons of the year, and the young fry, apparently of the same species, are sometimes very abundant there. Sir William says that for excellence and delicacy of flavour this fish cannot be surpassed, being considered superior to the common herring of Scotland, and that, preserved in oil in the manner of sardines, it would eclipse even those delicacies.

In respect to the value of these fishes from an economic point of view, Sir William Macleay remarks that it is certain that, so far as the immediate vicinity of Sydney is concerned, the two species referred to, as well as some others of perhaps less note, annually in the winter seasons pass the Heads, proceeding in a northerly direction in enormous shoals. That these fishes are of great value as food, and that they might be utilised to an almost unlimited extent in various ways, scarcely admit of question. The establishment, however, of a new industry, such as a herring fishery, in New South Wales, would be a difficult and costly thing, and could not be undertaken with hope of immediate returns. He instances the British Fishery Society, established about the end of the last century for the prosecution of the herring fishery in the north of Scotland, which laboured for many years before it became a complete success, though for a long time it was largely assisted by the Government with grants, bounties, &c. So likewise, he says, it must be here before much can be done. In the absence of Government aid or the resources of a wealthy company ready to undertake the establishment of fisheries on our shores, all that can be attempted is the endeavour to acquire an aquaintance with the history and habits of the finny tribes. Sir William concludes his remarks on the interesting subject of a possible herring fishery in New South Wales with the very practical suggestion that all those who have opportunities, such as fishermen, masters of coasting vessels, &c., should make notes of *where* and *when* they came across shoals of fish; the kinds of fish, of which a specimen or two should be placed in spirits for identification; the *direction* in which the shoals were moving; the apparent extent of them; whether the fish were full or spent; and of any other items occurring to the observer at the time.

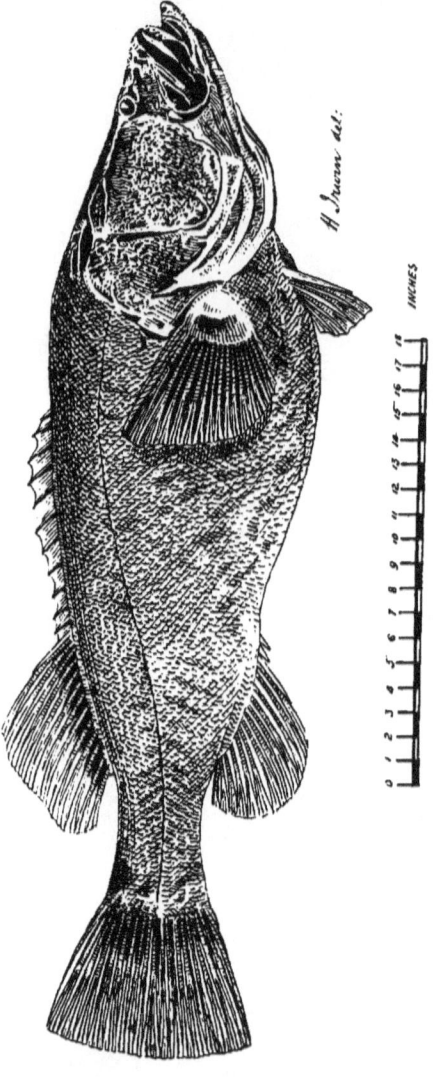

MURRAY COD. *Oligorus macquariensis.*

Attains a weight of 120 lbs.

CHAPTER II.

INLAND WATERS FISHERIES.

THE inland or fresh-water fisheries, as compared with those on the seaboard, are of but small importance. With the exception of the river system embraced in the Murray, Murrumbidgee, Lachlan, and Darling Rivers, which reach the sea in the colony of South Australia; Lake George, in the counties of Argyle and Murray, a magnificent sheet of water some 22 miles in length by 8 in breadth; and the few large rivers such as the Richmond, the Clarence, the Manning, the Hunter, the Shoalhaven, the Clyde, and others which take their rise in the eastern side of the main range, New South Wales, from a fisheries point of view, may be regarded as practically waterless. It is not, therefore, to be expected that our fresh-water fishes can be numerous outside the influence of waters I have enumerated; and in the far western country a fish is never seen. The principal fresh-water fish we possess is the Murray Cod, a fish really of the perch family (*Oligorus Macquariensis*) being the "Kookoobul" of the Murrumbidgee aboriginals, and the "Pundy" of those on the Lower Murray. There are two species of this genus, which belongs to the family of the perches. It is very voracious devouring everything in the shape of fish or animal which its enormous jaws can compass. It is a most excellent fish for the table, and has been known to reach a weight of 120 lb. The young fish are to be found in the billabongs and at the heads of streams, the adult fish lower down. They seem to have their periods of migration, ascending the streams in summer and descending them in winter, but as they thrive well in Lake George where they cannot make their ascent and descent, their propagation and development are evidently not dependent upon facilities of migration. Quite a considerable trade in this fish has been established with the neighbouring colony and Victoria. The principal catch in this connection is made in the Murray River, in the vicinity of the border town of Moama. It may be estimated that during the last eight years this river supplied an average of 90,000 lb. weight of this fish to the Melbourne market. In one of the earlier of these years cod to the enormous weight of 330,000 lb. were captured, but since the appointment of inspectors at points along the river the supply has been kept somewhat in check. Had this not been done the species might by this time have become extinct, for it is beyond reason to suppose that any stream, however prolific, could withstand continually such an enormous drain upon its resources. The supply of this cod to the New South Wales metropolis has not been nearly so abundant. The Murray River is too remote from Sydney to admit of supplies reaching their destination in good condition under the present arrangements of transit, so that our metropolis has to be dependent principally upon the catches made on the Macquarie and Darling Rivers, in direct railway communication with the seaboard. It would be quite possible to establish a lucrative trade between Lake George and Sydney. The lake teems with this fish, but so far only two or three fishermen pursue their vocation there, and their catch being greedily snapped up by the residents of the neighbouring towns, often at really excessive prices, seldom has a chance of reaching Sydney.

Lake George, 2,129 feet above the sea-level, is a magnificent sheet of water, 22 miles in length by an average width of 7 miles, and has a mean depth of 8 feet.

In the year 1854 the lake was practically dry, consisting of only a chain of ponds. It received its water in the great flood of 1862, and has maintained itself in more or less volume ever since. At the present time it abounds with cod. The presence of this fish is due to the circumstance of Mr. (afterwards Sir) Terence Aubrey Murray having succeeded in transporting some fry of this fish from the Murrumbidgee River to the Wandradene Ponds and Lagoons on his estate at Collector, on the northern boundary of the lake.

During the flood alluded to the water from these ponds overflowed into the lake basin, carrying with it large numbers of the fish, which by that time had become very prolific. These fish have continued to breed comparatively undisturbed ever since, and they now exist in large numbers,

TRAMMEL NET. END VIEW.

TRAMMEL NET. SIDE VIEW.

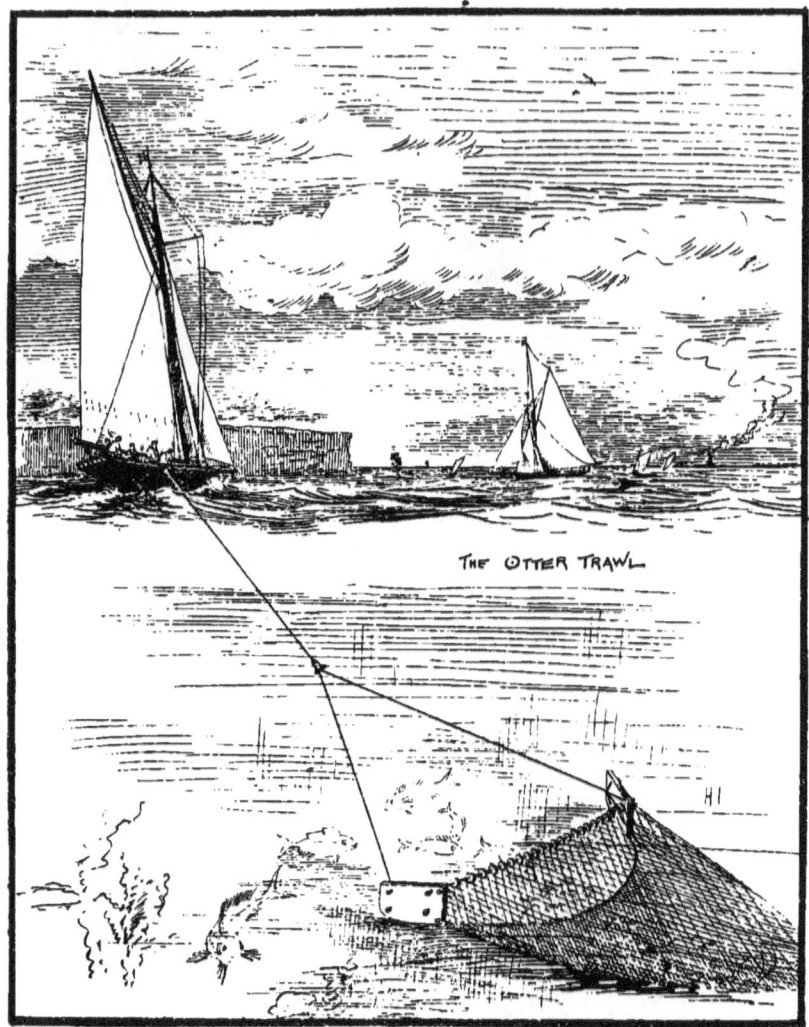
THE OTTER TRAWL

and of all weights and sizes. There is vacant here a field for successful enterprise to men who would enter upon the business with proper appliances; those now in use on the lake are crude in the extreme.

They consist of a very indifferently hung net, and a bultow or long line, to which are attached snoods about a foot in length furnished with hooks; these, when baited with meat, chrysalis, grub, or other tempting morsel are lowered into the water, moored, and left for some hours, very frequently all night. A fish when hooked at once succumbs and remains quiescent until the fisherman returns some hours later to overhaul the line and collect his catch; the fish are usually lifted into the boat with a scoop net. The centre of the lake is almost a dead level, and being free from obstructions would seem to suit the use of the otter trawl which might be employed with advantage, as also might the trammel net. With such instruments as these the lake could be made to yield in profusion of the abundant stores it undoubtedly holds.

The next important fresh-water fish is the Golden Perch or Yellow Belly. There are two species of this fish (*Ctenolates ambiguus* and *C. Christyi*). The first of these is common in all the fresh-water creeks and rivers; it is of a delicate flavour, rich, and attains a weight of 7 lb. Its time and manner of spawning are the same as the Murray cod. The fish itself, too, is very beautiful in appearance. The body is of a magnificent green, the sides and behind the dorsal are rich golden, the head is a beautiful mixture of green, purple, yellow, and scarlet, with fine golden tinges. The belly is white, the dorsal fin purplish-green, anal scarlet with a yellow base and purple end, pectorals scarlet on their bases and yellow in their second half, the eye purple with an interior white ring. The whole assumes a blending of rich colour which is really difficult to conceive, much less is it possible to convey an adequate idea of it by bare description.

The silver perch or bream (*Therapon richardsonii*) is another fish of extremely rich and delicate flavour, and attains a weight of 5 lb. or 6 lb. It is usually captured by means of a net, the small size of its mouth preventing its taking the hook commonly used. There are several species of this genus in Australian waters, but they do not call for special comment.

The blackfish (*Gadopsis marmoratus*) is common to our rivers generally. Ichthyologically regarded, this fish is a curiosity, being, according to Professor M'Coy, a type between the thorny-finned and soft-finned fishes. It is a mud fish generally obtained by emptying waterholes when made low by the summer heat. It is rich and oily, but a good table fish, and is readily caught with a line.

The catfish, belonging to the genus *Siluridæ*, is abundant in the back waters and lagoons in the western country. It is claimed to be an excellent fish, and is in great request in those localities where other species are scarce. It is fat and eel-like in flavour, but its appearance is not by any means inviting. When full grown it averages 2 feet in length.

The bony bream (*chatoessus richardsonii*), a fish of the herring tribe, is found in the western rivers. It is called *Ka-i-ra* by the Murrumbidgee natives. It appears at times in immense shoals. It is a handsome fair-sized fish, but owing to numberless bones it contains it is not utilised for food purposes. Another species of this fish (*C. erebi*) forms in its season one of the principal articles of food of the aboriginals on the Darling. A peculiar feature in connection with its use is that the young women are not allowed to partake of it from a belief that if they did all the fishes would die. It is also placed on the tops of graves from superstitious ideas. These statements are offered for what they may be worth. In making them it is proper to say that the late Sir William Macleay considered they had no foundation in fact. Apropos of this legend, if such it be, the writer is induced to record what is positively asserted to be a fact in connection with the Murrumbidgee Cod—it is that they carry the picture of the tree under which they were spawned; and the following is given as the method of opening the fish to obtain the view of the oak, gum, or other object near to which the fish, being operated upon, began its existence. Lay the fish on his port or left side, that is with his back fin towards the right hand, then cut from the tail close along the backbone as far as the first rib, cut the first rib through, but be careful not to disturb a very thin transparent skin, something like tissue paper. If necessary, spring a few more of the ribs and pull the fish asunder, the picture of the tree will then be exposed in the skin on which, if carefully removed and spread on a sheet of paper it will be more plainly seen. The writer has not yet verified this statement—possibly some curious reader may be inclined himself to test its correctness by experiment.

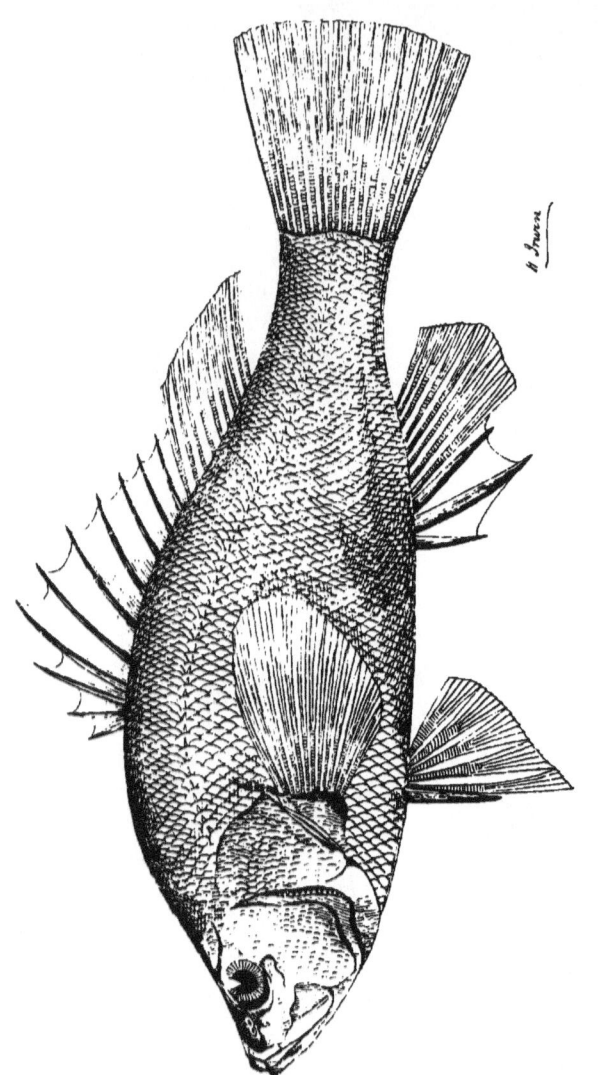

GOLDEN PERCH. *Ctenolates ambiguus.*
Attains a weight of 7 lbs.

So far reference has been made more especially to the fishes of the western waters. Those of the eastern rivers are of a less exclusively fresh-water character. The principal is the perch (*Lates colonorum*) frequently found in salt-water; the mullet (*Mugil dobula*) visiting the sea annually after attaining the adult state; also the eel (*Anguilla australis*) and the herring (*Clupea novæ hollandiæ*) are all frequently found in the salt water. These four species are in all the rivers of the east coast, and are all good fish. In the Clarence and Richmond Rivers there are found an additional mullet (*Mugil petardi*), an additional perch (*Lates curtus*), and, what is considered remarkable, two of the fishes of the Murray system, the cod and the cat-fish. The fact of the cod being found in the Clarence seems to offer proof that its acclimatisation to all the eastern rivers, a point at one time very much doubted, is well within the bounds of possibility. These, with a few other species of quite minor importance, may be said to constitute the whole of the fresh-water fish fauna of New South Wales. The list is not a long one, and it will be readily understood that minute legislation to protect these fisheries did not seem to be needed, and so the "Fisheries Act, 1881," did not enter largely into its regulation; it simply prescribed the size of mesh to be used in netting fish, and stipulated that the net should not be set wholly across a stream. It gave no power to close waters against the use of fishing-nets, nor did it require fishermen to take out licenses or ensure the protection of introduced fish.

The enormous drain which took place in supplying the Victorian market with cod from the Murray at last brought the importance attaching to inland fisheries under public notice, and resulted in Mr. J. M. Chanter, M.P., introducing a Bill to Parliament which eventuated in the enactment of the "Inland Waters Fisheries Act, 1887." This Act cured some of the evils that had been complained of; it legalised the closing of waters against net-fishing, enlarged the size of the mesh to be used, gave protection to non-indigenous fish, and in other ways assisted in improving the fisheries. Until, however, some arrangement shall have been agreed upon by the two colonies—Victoria and New South Wales—there will always be a difficulty about protecting fish in the Murray River. This river being wholly within the Colony of New South Wales, so the protection of its piscine wealth is wholly within its jurisdiction; but as the southern bank of the river is within the Victorian area the fisherman of Victoria may net the river from his own bank, and unless the New South Wales Inspector happens to be on the spot and has conveniences for taking the portion of the offending fisherman's net, which may be still in the water, he can get off scot free, and in no case can the fisheries inspector touch him if he is on Victorian ground. Occasion was taken by the Fisheries Commission of this Colony to invite the Government of Victoria to assist in putting down this abuse, but the Victorian powers declined to interfere, and so the evil still exists. Better counsels will, however, it is expected, prevail, for as I am writing on this subject, I have had placed in my hands a Victorian paper from which it appears that the fisheries industry is being taken up by the Parliament of that colony, and amongst other proposals it is suggested that the New South Wales Fisheries Inspector ought to be appointed for the Victorian side as well. This suggestion is very similar to the one proposed to Victoria only a short time previously and rejected.

FISH ACCLIMATISATION.

One of the first, if not the first, successful attempt to introduce new fish into New South Wales was made in 1888, by Messrs. John Gale and F. Campbell, of Queanbeyan. These gentlemen proceeded to Ballaarat, in Victoria, and obtained from the Acclimatisation Society there three hundred yearling trout from 3 to 5 inches long, eighty English perch, and forty Russian carp. By untiring exertion, during a long and tedious journey, occupying over thirty hours, partly by rail and partly by coach, they were successful in reaching Queanbeyan, with all but forty of the fish alive, and the loss of these forty was evidently accidental. The perch and carp were placed in waters near Queanbeyan. About half of the trout yearlings were distributed in the Cotter, Queanbeyan, Molonglo, Yass, and Naas Rivers, and the remainder in the Little River, in the Braidwood District, 34 miles further on, and in stream tributaries of the Snowy River, in the Monaro District, 100 miles further on. Subsequent investigations by these enterprising gentlemen go to show that in the Queanbeyan River the trout have bred marvellously, specimens weighing from 3 lb. to $5\frac{1}{2}$ lb. having

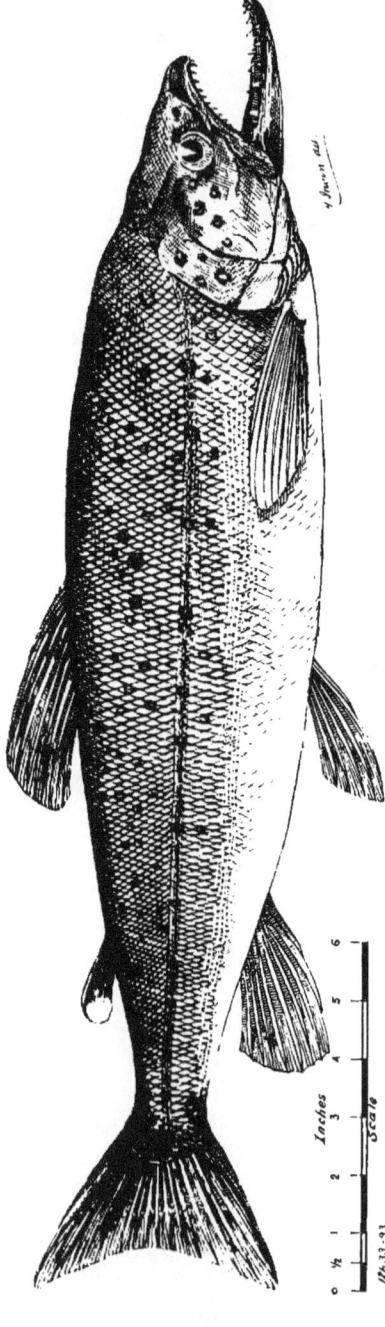

TROUT. Taken in the Molonglo River.

been captured, that the Cotter River is teeming with them, and that from thence they are entering the Murrumbidgee River. While they record no results from the Yass and Naas Rivers, they report that in the second year after the liberation of the parent fish in the Little and Snowy Rivers, experiments they made resulted in the netting of some hundreds of small fish.

Some eighteen months since a trout over 2 feet in length, very probably one of the yearlings brought over from Ballaarat, was found by Mr. N. Lockyer, of the Colonial Treasury Department, stranded on the banks of the Molonglo River. Mr. Lockyer kindly presented this trout to the writer, who had it attractively mounted and displayed at the recent Tasmanian Exhibition as a specimen of the rapid growth which, under favourable conditions, trout can attain in New South Wales. [*See* illustration.]

An interesting account of the journey from Ballaarat, written by Mr. Gale, will be found in the appendices.

The acclimatisation of several of the species of American Salmonidæ was a matter which the writer took opportunity to bring under the notice of the Fisheries Commissioners. He proposed to introduce the Californian salmon (*Salmo quinnat*), the schoodic salmon (*Salmo sebago, var. salar*), and the Californian or rainbow trout (*salmo irideus*). Some of the characteristics of these fish are hardiness, greater vitality, more rapid growth, and a capability to develop in waters of a comparatively high temperature, such as would certainly be fatal to some other species of the Salmonidæ. Each of these characteristics seemed to point to these species as eminently suitable to New South Wales waters. The proposal advanced to a certain stage, the supply of the ova having been undertaken by the American Consul, G. W. Griffin, when circumstances arose to prevent the experiment from being carried into effect. Since that attempt, however, the common brown trout (*Salmo fario*) has been on repeated occasions successfully hatched from ova supplied from New Zealand and Victoria, as well as a few Loch Leven (*Salmo levenensis*) and brook trout (*Salmo fontinalis*), and liberated in the early fry stage in the various suitable streams. The temperature of Sydney, however, proved too high to allow of the growth of the fry to the yearling stage, but in order to accomplish this a proposal has been under consideration to erect a fish hatchery on the elevated plateau at Berrima, some 80 miles distant from the metropolis. The Wingecarribee River, a permanent stream, which takes its rise in an extensive series of swamps supplied from an enormous catchment area, flows past the hatchery site and maintains a comparatively low temperature right through the summer months. There is abundant reason to expect that the culture of non-indigenous fresh-water fish of various kinds could be carried on there with every probability of success.

About two years since the writer made the experiment of travelling trout fry to the several streams assigned to them in jars about three parts filled with water and hermetically sealed. This mode of transmission proved so successful that at Sydney it has quite superseded the old method of forwarding in open jars. Fry can be sent in the jars for any reasonable distance. After determining by actual experiment that it would exist so imprisoned for seventy-two hours, the method was still further tested by shipping to Wellington, New Zealand, some fry of the ova which originally had been sent thence and hatched out in New South Wales. The attempt proved successful, and in like manner the experiment was repeated between Wellington and Sydney.

MARINE AND FRESH WATER PISCICULTURE.

In respect to marine and fresh water fish culture proper, not much has yet been attempted. Part 3 of the Fisheries Act, 1881, was evidently framed under the idea that if proper inducements were offered to freeholders and leaseholders of land suitable for the purpose, they would enter upon the establishment of artificial marine fisheries, but that part of the Act has so far proved a dead letter. The coast, however, abounds with lakes and lagoons, the property of the Crown, which could easily be made accessible to the influx and efflux of the tides; if the Bill to regulate the fisheries elsewhere noticed in this pamphlet becomes law, these and other suitable waters will be available to the public for lease for general fisheries purposes. It will probably be necessary for the Government to take the matter up in the first instance, in order to show what can be done in the shape of marine fish culture, and there are many places at which experiments in this direction can be carried out at quite inconsiderable cost—one exceptionally suitable place, at Lake Macquarie, may be mentioned. On the southern shore of the channel

The Hatching Site, Wingecarribee River.

entrance a line of tramway has been constructed across the mouth of a bay for the purpose of conveying ballast to the breakwater at the Heads. This viaduct, while it encloses perhaps 200 acres of water, provides communication with the tide through a bridge 100 feet long—the water already teems with fish fry of various kinds, thus proving its suitability as a nursery and feeding ground. The propriety of setting it apart for the purposes of experiment and observation in the propagation of fish, and perhaps crustacea and mollusca too, will be obvious. Some few large estate proprietors back from the coast have certainly introduced trout and other fresh water non-indigenous fish into their own artificially conserved waters, but no extensive or general movement in this direction has taken place.

It must not, however, be concluded that marine fish culture, such as is here suggested, will apply to all species of marine fish—scientific research has revealed the fact that in European waters certain species breed in the open sea; their ova, according to its specific gravity, finding a location either on the surface, or at various gradations of depth, or on the ocean bottom. It would be difficult perhaps to control such species within the limits of enclosed tidal waters, at least those of them which pass their whole lives at sea; but some, the sole for instance, and indeed the *pleuronectidæ* generally, gravitate at quite an early age towards the quieter waters of bays and inlets, and remain there until they reach the adult stage, when in turn they seek the sea and perform their office of reproduction.

To what extent Australian fish species are subject to this routine is not known, such can only be determined by systematic observation and experiment, and these have not yet been attempted.

But in this connection Mr. Alexander Oliver, in an article on the "Correlation of the inlets to the migratory and other species of our sea fishes," affirms that the red bream, the progeny of the schnapper, generally hatched at sea, becomes from its cock schnapper period a denizen of inlets until, in a more adult stage, it reaches out again to the ocean depths.

This similarity of habit between at least one principal species of Australian fish and many of the edible fishes of the Northern Hemisphere is interesting in the extreme.

The value of authentic knowledge respecting the life history and habits of our food fishes can scarcely be over-estimated.

Mr. Oliver's paper will be found amongst the Appendices.

CHAPTER III.

THE FISHERIES LAWS.

UNTIL the year 1865 no attempt had been made to bring the fisheries under legislative enactment. With splendid disregard of future requirements, seine-hauling had been carried on at will with nets of all lengths, and composed of meshes so small that the resultant destruction began to tell seriously on the supply and to attract public attention. Fishermen could at that time follow their avocations only in Port Jackson, Botany, George's River, and Broken Bay. Waters further afield, such as Lake Macquarie, Port Stephens, Lake Illawarra, &c., were, through the absence of facilities for transit, completely closed to them, and to such an extent were the available waters becoming depopulated, that some of the more intelligent fishermen, at last awaking to the position, and fearing that the future prosecution of their calling was in danger, joined with the public voice in seeking legislative protection. The aid of Mr. Richard Driver, junior, a Member of the Legislative Assembly, was invoked to bring the matter before Parliament. The result was a reference of it to a Select Committee of the House for consideration. The witnesses, many of whom were practical fishermen, all declared to the absolute necessity for protection to the fisheries. The Committee elicited from witnesses that it was quite the general custom for fishermen to work with nets composed of a three-quarters of an inch mesh, the effect of which was to land and destroy enormous quantities of fry, and that to a very large extent the depletion of the fishing-grounds was due to that practice. It was also shown that a still more complete mode of spoliation had been in operation, and that was a system popularly known as "stalling." It consisted of shooting at high tide a net of some 250 to 300 or more of fathoms across a shallow bay or around flats, and leaving it until the receding tide had left the enclosure dry. By this means tons upon tons of fish were destroyed, and as from these quantities only those of a saleable size and of the more choice species were selected, the large remainder of the stranded fish was left unused and to rot on the beaches, whither for the most part it would be carried by the next flow of tide. It will be quite easy to imagine the extent of the destruction and waste thus created. The culpability of these effective processes of extermination was readily admitted, but the plea urged in extenuation was that while one section of the fishermen practised them the other section had to do likewise. The outcome of the labours of the Select Committee was the enactment of the Fisheries Act 1865, which came to be popularly known as Dick Driver's Act. This Act made a division of the year into winter and summer months and specified the description of nets to be used during the period of each division, and in order to put a check on the "stalling" system it made it a penal offence to fix or stake any net within a mile of the shore, or at the mouth of any river. The administration was entrusted to the Police and Customs Departments, but the oversight bestowed does not seem to have been very stringent, for in a short time fishermen began to resume the practice of stalling, only contenting themselves with taking necessary precautions to avoid detection. In the year 1880, however, the fisheries question was taken up in real earnest by the Government of the day, Sir Henry Parkes, K.C.M.G., being the Premier, when a Royal Commission, under the Presidency of the Honorable William Macleay, M.L.C., and composed of gentlemen scientifically and practically qualified for the task, was appointed to inquire into the marine and fresh water fisheries and oyster fisheries of the Colony, and to advise of the best means for developing and preserving them. This Commission did its work so well and so thoroughly and collected such valuable and complete information about the resources and possibilities of the fisheries that it merits grateful remembrance by every one professing interest in the advancement of the Colony's industries. Nothing at all equal to the information or the suggestions which the Commission's report contains and which is largely quoted from throughout this pamphlet had ever before been collected or published, and the value thereof can scarcely be too highly rated or appreciated. So intimately indeed does work of this Royal Commission seem to have become identified with the subsequent progress and development of the fisheries that the present publication would be incomplete indeed if it failed to accord very special tribute to the result of its labours. As a means of officially perpetuating a record of the names of the gentlemen who rendered such signal service, it has been thought fitting to incorporate a copy of the Commission appointing them:—

Commission.

VICTORIA, by the Grace of God, of the United Kingdom of Great Britain and Ireland, Queen, Defender of the Faith, and so forth.—

To our trusty and well-beloved—

The Honorable WILLIAM MACLEAY, a Member of our Legislative Council of our Colony of New South Wales ; JAMES CHARLES COX, Esquire, Doctor of Medicine ; The Honorable WILLIAM BEDE DALLEY, Q.C., a Member of our said Legislative Council ; HENRY CARY DANGAR, Esquire, Barrister-at-Law ; RICHARD DRIVER, Esquire, a Member of our Legislative Assembly of our said Colony ; JAMES SQUIRE FARNELL, Esquire, a Member of our said Legislative Assembly ; RICHARD HILL, Esquire, one of our Justices of the Peace of our said Colony ; FRANCIS HIXSON, Esquire, R.N., President of the Marine Board of our said Colony ; The Honorable THOMAS HOLT, a Member of our said Legislative Council ; ALEXANDER OLIVER, Esquire, Barrister-at-Law ; EDWARD PIERSON RAMSAY, Esquire, Curator of the Australian Museum ; CHARLES CARLETON SKARRATT, Esquire, a Justice of the Peace of our said Colony ; The Honorable GEORGE THORNTON, a Member of our said Legislative Council ; and GEORGE FREDERICK WANT, Esquire ;

Greeting :

Know ye that We, reposing great trust and confidence in your ability, zeal, and industry, discretion and integrity, do by these presents authorise and appoint you, or any three or more of you, as hereinafter mentioned, to make a diligent and full investigation into the actual state and prospect of the Fisheries of our said Colony ; the best means of developing and preserving them ; the expediency of encouraging pisciculture, or of supplementing the natural supply by the introduction and acclimatisation of useful foreign species and upon all matters bearing upon the above-mentioned subject : And We do by these presents give and grant to you, or any three or more of you, at any meeting or meetings to which all of you shall have been duly summoned, full power and authority to call before you all such persons as you may judge necessary, by whom you may be better informed of the truth in the premises, and to require the production of all such books, papers, writings, and all other documents as you may deem expedient, and to visit and inspect the same at the offices or places where the same or any of them may be deposited, and to inquire of the premises by all lawful ways and means : And Our further will and pleasure is that you, or any three or more of you, after due examination of the premises, do and shall, within the space of four months after the date of this our Commission, or sooner if the same can reasonably be, certify to Us, in the Office of the Colonial Secretary, under your, or any three or more of your hands and seals, what you shall find touching the premises : And We hereby command all Government Officers and other persons whomsoever within our said Colony that they be assistant to you and each of you in the execution of these presents: And we appoint you, the said WILLIAM MACLEAY, Esquire, to be President of this our Commission.

 In testimony whereof, We have caused these our Letters to be made Patent, and the Great Seal of our said Colony to be hereunto affixed.

  Witness our right, trusty, and well-beloved Councillor, SIR AUGUSTUS WILLIAM FREDERICK SPENCER LOFTUS (commonly called LORD AUGUSTUS LOFTUS), Knight Grand Cross of our Most Honorable Order of the Bath, our Governor and Commander-in-Chief of our Colony of New South Wales and its Dependencies, at Government House, Sydney, in New South Wales aforesaid, this sixth day of January, in the year of our Lord one thousand eight hundred and eighty, and in the forty-third year of our Reign.

         AUGUSTUS LOFTUS.
    By His Excellency's Command,
         HENRY PARKES.

Entered on record by me, in REGISTER OF PATENTS, No. 10, pages 151-9, this eighth day of January, one thousand eight hundred and eighty.
       CRITCHETT WALKER
   (For the Colonial Secretary and Registrar of Records).

 The outcome of the report of this Royal Commission was the Fisheries Act of 1881, elsewhere cursorily referred to in relation to its enactments for the control of the Oyster Fisheries. In moving the second reading of the Bill Sir Henry Parkes said :

 I may explain that the Bill is framed with the intention of carrying out the main recommendations of the Commission which sat last year to inquire into the state of the fisheries of the Colony, and to suggest measures for their development and general improvement. The Commission, it will be recollected, was composed of gentlemen, all of whom had, more or less, a practical knowledge of fishing, several of them having devoted themselves for many years to the pursuit; and they fairly represented different classes of society—men who fished for sport as well as men who followed the pursuit as a means of livelihood. Altogether I think the Commission embraced nearly the whole available talent in the Colony for investigating the subject. Their report, which was very carefully prepared, and which may be well described as a very valuable document, went thoroughly into the state of our fisheries, of our supplies of fish, from a food point of view, and they suggested with great minuteness various steps to be taken for the better preservation of the supplies and for the better regulation of the fisheries. The present measure is substantially the outcome of their investigation. The Bill which I have the honour to ask the House to read the second time proposes the new machinery for the management of the fisheries, and it makes provision for the objects which are to be attained by this machinery. It proposes to repeal existing Acts and a portion of the Land Act which now empowers the Minister for Lands to grant leases. Then it proposes to vest the control of our fisheries for the future in six unpaid Commissioners; after which it goes on to make provision for the appointment of the necessary officers—a secretary and inspectors—to carry out the arrangements of the Commissioners as far as the fisheries are concerned. The Bill also provides that the police, and officers of the Marine Board holding office in remote localities, shall act as assistant inspectors, in order more economically to carry out inspection on remote rivers, inlets, and harbours. The fishery waters are to be divided into three distinct grounds. There is to be the home fishery, the northern fishery, and the southern fishery; and the Bill empowers the Commissioners to make the necessary regulations for their protection. Although I believe that we cannot lay claim to anything like the rich sources of supply which some other countries possess, still I think our fish supplies are far more rich and valuable than is generally supposed. It cannot be for a moment doubted that an enormous waste goes on by the destruction of spawn and young fish—a waste which is altogether beyond any calculation in excess of the mere diminution of our fish supplies by the consumption of the fish as an article of food. The Commissioners make some reference in their report to the destruction of fish which is constantly going on, and I will trouble the House with one or two short extracts from it. On page 33 the report says—

" With an extensive sea-board, an apparently unlimited supply of fish, and a very limited consumption, it might naturally be supposed that for many years to come legislation for the preservation of the fisheries of New South Wales would be premature and unnecessary. Experience, however, tells a very different tale. It is undoubted that in and about Port Jackson, Botany Bay, Broken Bay, and the Lakes Macquarie and Tuggerah, and indeed at every place easily reached by the Sydney fisherman, the quantity of fish has fallen off enormously of late years, and is continuing to do so. If this were due to the legitimate exhaustion of the supply by its use for food, or indeed for any useful purpose, there would be less reason for regret or interference; but the fact being that the quantity of fish caught and consumed has never at any time been sufficient of itself to affect to any appreciable degree the supply, and that the diminution which is going on in the supply of some of our best fishes is due entirely to the wanton destruction by fishermen of the spawn and young, indicates a state of things which demands immediate legislative interference."

To show the enormous extent to which the destruction of this very valuable article of food may go, I will quote a reference made by the report to another part of the world—a part of the world which like ours has a new population. Alluding to the Sacramento and Columbia Rivers, the report says—

" There is not a salmon river in Europe that does not annually liberate a much larger number of artificially-reared fish than the annual catch, and the process has been adopted and carried out most successfully on the western coasts of North America, a country newer to European advancement and civilisation even than we are ourselves. The many millions of large salmon annually tinned or canned on the Sacramento and Columbia Rivers seem not as yet to affect the supply, but we find from a report of the Commissioners of Californian fisheries for 1878 and 1879 that in the Sacramento River the supply is amply kept up by the annual hatching and liberation of 2,500,000 young fish. It is probable that the same effectual mode of preventing exhaustion of the supply is employed on the Columbia, where a still greater number of the adult fish are utilised and canned and often eaten here as English salmon."

I make this quotation to show that even where fish are caught in very large quantities and exported to all parts of the world as food, where this process of consumption is rapidly going on, still it is easy to raise the supply far in excess of the destruction caused by this mercantile use of fish. But if, instead of making any provision whatever to keep up the supply of fish, we from neglect allow the needless destruction of young fish and spawn, our supplies according to this report will very soon dwindle away, and fish will become a rare commodity in our markets. I have one other quotation to make from the Commissioners' report. Under the head of "Protection of our Fisheries" they say—

"We have pointed out the destruction at present constantly occurring of the young fish and the spawn, and we recommend for their protection that a close season shall extend from 1st April to 1st October in each year, in which the use of all nets shall be prohibited within any bay, lake, or inlet of the coast, unless specially exempted by proclamation in the *Government Gazette*; that during the other six months the mesh of the nets used shall not be smaller than $1\frac{1}{2}$ inch, measured diagonally, and that no prawn-net shall be permitted to be used of greater length than fifteen fathoms. We also advise that where fixed or stake nets are used for the capture of fish they should be prohibited from being stretched completely across any creek, river, or inlet, and that the minimum size of the mesh should be four inches."

The second part of the Bill gives power to grant leases under proper regulations, and provides that in all cases fishing-boats shall be licensed. Licenses are also to be issued for making private oyster-beds, and likewise for dredging and for dealing in oysters. Penalties are also provided for burning the oysters for the mere purpose of obtaining the lime—a practice which is carried on extensively—and provision is made for the use of proper appliances for the sea-carriage of oysters. Through inadvertence I have given a description of the provisions of the Bill relating to the oyster fisheries a little earlier than I intended. With regard to the fish generally, the Bill provides that a close season shall exist for those fish, which are familiarly know to us as flathead, whiting, garfish, mullet, and so forth, extending from the beginning of April to the end of September. It then provides that the nets used shall have meshes of a width of not less than $1\frac{1}{2}$ inch, so that the small fish may escape. The meshes of stake nets are not to be less than 4 inches in width. Then there are penalties for the destruction of undersized fish, penalties to prevent the riddling of prawns except in proximity to the waters from which they are taken, so that the small fish caught in the prawn nets may be allowed to escape. There are provisions for many other things. It is provided that in future no explosives shall be used for the purpose of destroying fish. I have briefly explained the general provisions of the measure, and I think that honourable members will not hesitate to read the Bill a second time, and to lend their assistance to improve its provisions in Committee.

This Bill engaged the attention of Parliament from January to April, 1881, its provisions being debated with the keenest interest by a large number of the more prominent members both of the Legislative Assembly and Legislative Council. The Fisheries Act, 1881, with the exception of Part II relating to oyster fisheries, which has been repealed, is for the most part the law by which the fisheries are at present controlled, and it is, without doubt, the first formal attempt at comprehensive legislation based on the principle of protecting the natural supplies of fish, oysters, lobsters, and prawns, and of regulating and controlling their capture. The administrative authority, subject to the customary Executive control, is a body of five Commissioners appointed by the Governor-in-Council, whose term of office is five years, and whose jurisdiction extends over the entire territory. The fisheries on the seaboard are distributed into three divisions —the Home, the Northern, and the Southern fisheries; in one or other of which divisions every marine Fishery is contained. The regular supervision of these divisions is made the duty of inspectors and assistant inspectors; and, in addition to the regular staff, certain Government officials are, by the Act, created inspectors *ex officio*. The inspectors and assistant inspectors are required to report periodically to the Commissioners, as to the state of the fisheries included within their respective districts. Most extensive powers to frame regulations on all matters of detail are vested in the Governor-in-Council.

The chief protective, regulative, and penal provisions of the Act are shown in the subjoined summary:—

FISHING-NETS.

In all tidal-water fisheries, that is to say, all sea-fisheries on the coast, unless during the close months or where the fisheries are absolutely closed for an extended term against fishing-nets of every kind, a lawful net may be of a length sufficient to enclose a space of 300 yards measured along the corks, but must not have a mesh in the bunt less than $2\frac{1}{4}$ inches or 3 inches in each wing. But *bona fide* garfish nets, if used during the open months, or elsewhere than in a fishery absolutely closed, are not illegal if the mesh in each wing is not less than 2 inches, the bunt and wings being hung on the same cork and lead lines; but such garfish nets must not in the bunt exceed 30 fathoms in length, or have in the bunt a mesh less than $1\frac{1}{3}$ inch. Prawn nets are legal, under the same limitations as to time and place, if they do not exceed 15 fathoms in length, or do not have a mesh less than 1 inch.

Stalling is prohibited at all times and places, but *bona fide* meshing-nets not exceeding 60 fathoms in length, and not less than 4 inches in the mesh, are permitted if not set during the close months in any close fishery, or in any fishery absolutely closed against netting.

Drift nets and purse seines of any length or mesh may be used in the open sea, *i.e.*, outside the mouths or limits of any bay, river, or inlet.

For inland waters nets may be any length, but must not be less in the mesh than 3 inches, and must not be set wholly across a river or creek, but this restriction does not apply to nets used in private fisheries. These provisions have been modified by those of a later enactment—the Inland Waters Fisheries Act of 1887.

CLOSE SEASON FOR NET FISH.

The Act provides a close season extending from the first of April to the thirtieth of September in each year, during which nets may not be used in tidal waters proclaimed as closed, under penalty not exceeding £50, and not less than £10. Tidal waters within areas so proclaimed are termed "Close Fisheries."

CLOSED FISHERIES.

Net-fishing of any kind is illegal also in tidal waters proclaimed closed against net-fishing, for any specified period.

LICENSES.

A license for every fishing boat has to be taken out annually—the license fee being £1; but after the thirtieth of June the fee is reduced to 10s. for the remainder of the year.

Fishermen must also take out an annual license, subject to like reduction for the broken period of the year; the fee is 10s.

PRAWN-FISHING.

The riddling of prawns is only allowed while the prawns are alive.

In the river Hunter an annual close season is made absolute, and in any other river an annual close season extending from the first of June to the thirtieth of September may be established by proclamation.

TORPEDOES, DYNAMITE, &c.

The use of torpedoes, dynamite, or poisonous matter in any waters is prohibited under a penalty. The prohibition, however, does not extend to persons lawfully authorised to explode torpedoes or dynamite.

UNMARKETABLE FISH.

It is made unlawful to sell, or expose for sale, or be in possession of any fish under certain specified weights. The prohibition does not, however, extend to collectors, owners of private fisheries, persons in possession of fish not intended for sale, or aboriginals, under certain conditions.

PRIVATE FISHERIES.

It would appear that the position of a proprietor of land in this Colony who had artificially admitted tidal waters over land of which he was the owner, is surrounded with no little doubt, not only in his relation to the Crown but also to the public right of fishery and navigation to which it would seem that all Crown lands are subject before alienation, and to which, even on alienation, such lands seem to continue subject, so far at least as they are within the influence of the tides. An opportunity of relieving private landowners from this uncertainty is afforded by the introduction of the present Act; and the provisions contained in Part III of it represent an attempt to place the whole subject on a satisfactory footing for the future.

The private fisheries thereby authorised are limited to tidal water fisheries. The admission of tidal water to private property, through or over Crown lands (*i.e.*, foreshores) is the characteristic feature of the private fisheries contemplated by the Act; and this appropriation of what may be considered as one of the Crown's regalia, and the necessary interference with the shore, and the *jus publicum* thereover, were considered as the circumstances which justified the legislation proposed.

The legal effect of a license to establish a private fishery is to vest in the grantee and all persons claiming under him an exclusive right of stocking the fishery with fish of every description (including crustaceans and molluscs), and of taking all such fish so long as the license is in operation, *i.e.*, so long as the terms and conditions subject to which it is granted be faithfully complied with. Moreover the licensee is placed in a position to prosecute any persons who steal any fish from his fishery, or who trespass within its limits. The grant empowers him to cut a trench or passage through the shore and to construct a sluice to admit the tidal water to his fishery, and any public rights-of-way of navigation over his fishery, and of taking fish therein, are wholly abrogated by the grant. On the other hand certain obligations are cast on the grantee or proprietor of the fishery. He is required to construct and maintain substantial bridges of prescribed dimensions across any trenches or cuttings of the shore; also to mark the boundaries of the fishery by stakes or as prescribed by the regulations. A private fishery will pass as an incorporeal hereditament appurtenant to and with the ownership of the soil. Although not in terms granted as a franchise, it will more resemble a franchise than any other incorporeal hereditament. The licensee or grantee of the fishery will of course always remain liable to the Crown for the fulfilment of the conditions of the grant. The property in fish in a private fishery vests in the owner of the fishery prior to, and not merely after, capture as in the case of Common of Piscary. For further details the reader is referred to Part III of the Act itself.

LIMITS OF JURISDICTION.

The fourth section of the Fisheries Act, after declaring that the duty of protecting, developing, and regulating the public fisheries of the Colony shall be vested in the Commissioners appointed under the Act, enacts that the duties, powers, and authority of the Commissioners shall extend to the territorial limits of the Colony. Those limits are defined as follows:—On the northern boundary by a line extending from Point Danger, a short distance to the northward of the Tweed River, to the head waters of the Macintyre River, where the 29th parallel of south latitude impinges on that river; thence westward by that parallel to its intersection by the 141st meridian of east longitude; southward, along that meridian to the waters of the River Murray; and eastward by the southern bank of that river to a point where a straight line from Cape Howe touches the nearest source of that river.

The eastern limit of the coastal fisheries is, in conformity with established law regulating the coastal boundaries of maritime states, regarded as being confined to a range of one nautical league from the margin of the coast along its entire length from Point Danger on the north to Cape Howe on the south.

ADMINISTRATION OF THE FISHERIES ACT.

The first-appointed Commissioners of Fisheries for New South Wales were:

    William Bede Dalley, Q.C.,
    Henry Carey Dangar, M.P.,
    The Honorable William Macleay, M.L.C.,
    Alexander Oliver, M.A., and
    The Honorable George Thornton, M.L.C.

These gentlemen, with the Honorable (afterwards Sir) William Macleay as President, were selected by the Government of the day from the members of the Royal Commission already referred to. Possessing a perfect knowledge of the objects they were expected to achieve, they immediately entered upon their honorary and important duties, and proceeded to bring the machinery of the new Act into operation.

On their recommendation the tidal fisheries were distributed into three large divisions, to the general supervision of each of which an inspector was appointed, these officers in their turn being assisted by subordinate inspectors, whose duties were confined to the special oversight of some one of the more important fish and oyster-producing waters. In addition, the services of the Customs and Pilot officers stationed at outlying points along the coast were availed of to oversee any fishing operations which might be taking place there. These minor officers were required to report in full detail to the divisional inspectors every circumstance as it transpired, and the divisional inspectors in turn made periodical communication to the Commissioners. Each inspector had also special standing instructions to notice the movements and habits of the various kinds of useful fish; to report the existence of any source of pollution in the waters, or of any mortality, disease, or ill-condition of fish, mollusca, or crustacea. All these items of information, condensed through the medium of the divisional inspectors' reports, came under the consideration of the Commissioners, who thus fully seized of every item of information concerning the fisheries which had taken place along the entire length of the coast-line, were in a position to apply to any evils or abuses they found existing one or other of the remedies which the Act provided, or their own ripe experience suggested.

One of the first of these abuses which came under notice was the indiscriminate fishing being carried on in every water within reach of the metropolis. The Tuggerah Beach Lakes, Lake Macquarie, the Hawkesbury, Parramatta, George's and Port Hacking Rivers, with their respective tributaries and affluents, having each been depleted to an alarming extent by reason of the hitherto practically unrestricted use of the fishermen's nets and graballs, the Commission took the very judicious step of withdrawing large portions of each of these important fishing-grounds from the operations of netters. The wisdom of these reservations very soon became apparent in the shoals of young fish of all kinds which made their appearance throughout the thus net-restricted waters. This was the first effective step taken in New South Wales to secure a continuity of supply; its practice is continued to the present time. The next movement was to regulate the lengths of fishing-nets and the dimensions of the meshes according to the new law; but in order that this restriction should not press too heavily upon the fishermen, they were allowed to continue the use of the nets they possessed at the time for more than fifteen months from the date the Fisheries Act of 1881 was passed into law.

While thus providing for the recovery of the natural supplies of fish in all the waters which had been so completely fished out by improvident fishermen, the Commissioners were not unmindful of their obligations to develop the fish supply in other directions also. They induced the Government to import valuable fishing-gear, such as is used in England, America, and Norway, in order that their applicability to the waters of this Colony might be tested, and also that our fishermen might be instructed in the modes of fishing practised in those countries. The implements thus imported consisted of a purse-seine net, such as is used by the cod-fishers on the coast of Maine, North America; a trammel net of French origin, consisting of a loose net of small meshes or sheeting between two tighter nets of larger meshes called walling, and usually shot with the tide in the eddy of a large rock, also in sheltered bays and deep-water harbours. A collection of glass hooks and floats, as used by the fishermen on the Norwegian coast, a herring-net and otter trawl, and also a beam trawl-net, similar to the kind employed in the fisheries on the east coast of England. All these implements were displayed to the utmost advantage in the Garden Palace, an edifice of immense capacity, erected for the Great International Exhibition,

Sydney, 1879 and 1880. Unfortunately, this imposing structure was totally destroyed by fire on the morning of the 22 September, 1882, and with it this valuable collection of fishing implements, together with all the books and documents belonging to the Fisheries Department, which at the time was located in the building. Not very long after this calamitous occurrence the *personnel* of the Fisheries Board as originally constituted had completely changed, every one of its first-appointed members having retired. Their positions were, with two exceptions, filled by gentlemen who had been members of the Royal Commission before referred to. The Board thus formed, consisted of :—

Dr. James C. Cox, F.L.S., President, and
Messrs. George Frederick Want,
John H. Geddes,
Frederick A. Thomas, and
Edward Pierson Ramsay, F.L.S.

Since this the constitution of the Board has suffered many changes, not less than fifteen different appointments having at various times been made to it during the decade it has been in existence to fill vacancies which had been occasioned by the retirement of some one or other of its members; these changes are detailed in the appendices; the only members at that period still retaining their positions are Dr. James C. Cox, the President, and Mr. (now Doctor) Edward Pierson Ramsay.

The first important duty which engaged the attention of the newly constituted Board was the furtherance of arrangements for the proper representation of the Colony at the Great International Fisheries Exhibition, London, 1883. The Commissioners entered upon the prosecution of the this task with considerable apprehension, owing to the hitherto culpable neglect of the capabilities which New South Wales possessed, both as a fish and oyster-producing country. However they concentrated their best efforts upon the undertaking and succeeded to a degree far in advance of their expectations. The Commissioners attributed very much of the success achieved to the able arrangements made by their colleague, Mr. E. P. Ramsay, under whose charge the exhibits had been placed. It was recorded, through the Agent-General in this Colony, that our fisheries exhibits excited very great interest, especially the paintings of food-fishes and the fishes themselves; the model fishing-boat with its gear net and set of fishing-lines was also quite a centre of attraction; the whole display leading people to imagine that we had developed really extensive fisheries; nor, indeed, was less surpise expressed at the very limited materials and methods of capture. The large collection of oysters claimed the attention of American growers whose oyster-beds were beginning to show signs of decrease, and they threatened to come over and "rent a few hundred miles of our country." The collection embraced samples from no less than sixty-five principal beds, and included specimens of the mud oyster, the rock and drift oyster, and one or two rare species. It is gratifying to be able to record that the Court was on several occasions visited by the Prince and Princess of Wales, and by other members of the Royal family.

Reverting to duties lying nearer home, the Commissioners began to find that the Fisheries Act of 1881, the administration of which had fallen to them, was so far from perfect as to need material amendment, and they set themselves to the task of preparing a new measure, entitled the "Fisheries and Oyster Culture Bill." They claimed for this Bill that, so far as it particularly concerned the practical fisherman, its provisions were set out with a clearness of expression not always to be found in the existing statute, while at the same time it enacted a manifestly improved method of regulating the oyster fisheries. This Bill was duly presented to the Government of the day, but it never reached the stage of introduction to Parliament. The Commission further recommended a survey of the sea bottom being made, with the view to the initiation of trawling experiments.

About this time the very necessary restrictions which the Commissioners, acting under the authority of the law, had imposed upon the fishermen, by closing considerable portions of the fish-producing waters against the operations of netting, were beginning to be felt, and complaints against what was designated in some quarters as harsh and tyrannical action were loud and deep. Besides these restrictions, which compelled fishermen to go farther afield for their fish, the Commissioners found it necessary to wage warfare against the over-length nets, composed of meshes much below the prescribed dimensions, which many of the fishermen persisted in using, notwithstanding the liberal provisions in that regard which had been enacted for their convenience by the

Fisheries Act of 1881. After repeated warnings of the consequences which must follow the persistent use of these illegal instruments for the capture of fish, the Commissioners had left to them no alternative but to seize their nets, and otherwise bring the offending persons under the penalties of the law. Of course men who had hitherto considered the finny tribes in our harbours and rivers their legitimate and indeed absolute property might be pardoned for considering such prohibitory steps as really aggressive; self-interest and convenience prevented many of them from caring for, or even apprehending, the inevitable consequences which would follow the attempt to supply an ever-increasing population with fish under conditions so extravagant and so wasteful; but it was nevertheless the duty of the authorities to conserve this portion of the public estate by insisting upon the production of fish on lines more favourable to the economy and continuity of supply. So far, however, from appreciating these efforts, the fishermen succeeded in invoking the aid of Parliament to relieve them from some fancied hardships. They obtained a Select Committee of the Legislative Assembly, under the presidency of Mr. A. R. Fremlin, the member for Redfern, who, after the examination of witnesses, brought up a Report stating that the Fisheries Act, 1881, had not fulfilled the expectations of its framers; that it had lessened the supply of fish, placed unwise restrictions upon our important fisheries and worked very harshly and oppressively to those engaged in fishing for a livelihood, and recommending an extension of the lengths and a reduction in the sizes of meshes of the nets which might be used, and an alteration in the sizes of the fish which it should be legal to capture. The Select Committee concluded its labours on the 20th April; in the following May Sir Alexander Stuart, the Colonial Secretary at the time, introduced a Bill to Parliament to amend the Fisheries Act: it resulted in the enactment of the Fisheries Act Amendment Act, 1883. This Act allowed the dimensions of nets for use in tidal waters to be determined by regulations, and relieved offenders convicted under certain sections of the 1881 Act from the forfeiture of their unlawful nets, except in cases where a previous conviction had been recorded. Under the power thus conferred the gar-fish net was reduced from one and a half to one and a quarter inches. This Act, together with the principal Act, is the law by which the marine fisheries have since been controlled, and it has been regularly administered by the Commissioners up to the present time. Every care has been taken that the restrictions it enacts especially as regards closures of waters against the use of fishing-nets, as well as its provisions respecting lengths and dimensions of nets and netting, shall be observed; but the task has proved a difficult one; the charms which forbidden waters appeared to have for the fishermen seemed too good for resistance, and the efforts of the Fisheries Inspectors, no matter how industriously and wisely directed, have not infrequently proved insufficient to baffle the everwatchful offenders and their folk, who have always stoutly contended that they are perpetually hampered in the profitable prosecution of their calling by the undue pressure of harsh and ill-advised legislation, unjustly administered by a Commission of gentlemen, some of whom have not a practical knowledge of the fisheries question. Setting aside these severe strictures upon its administration, this seems a rather sweeping condemnation of the comprehensive system of legislation on the fisheries, which in 1881 had been ushered in with so much trumpet flourish, and which seemed so pregnant with possibilities of the most promising nature; but the assertions were pressed with such force and persistency, and the complaints were discussed with so much vigour in the public press, that eventually the matter was again brought forward in Parliament, through the instrumentality of Mr. Frank Farnell, one of the members for Central Cumberland, and a son of the late Honorable J. S. Farnell, whose efforts in past years, more particularly in the development of oyster culture, had been so prominent. Mr. Frank Farnell, in his place in Parliament, assailed the Fisheries Commission for want of practical knowledge, and the officers under them for their administration of the Act; urged the abolition of the Board and the re-establishment of the department under direct Ministerial control. Sir Henry Parkes, Colonial Secretary, pointed out to the House that no administrative authority of such a kind as the Fisheries Commission could be of any value unless it gave widespread dissatisfaction, and that it indeed could not possibly satisfy persons who desired irregularly to fish in waters closed against them. Nevertheless, as he was by no means satisfied with the working of the Board, and as the Fisheries Act had been sufficiently long in existence for its working to be made manifest by proper inquiry, he did not think it was his duty to oppose the Select Committee for which Mr. Farnell was pressing; nor did he in any way complain of the proposed composition of it. He thought the inquiry would be conducted honestly, and that the mover, in making it, would be doing good to the country.

Accordingly a Select Committee, consisting of the undermentioned members of the Legislative Assembly, was appointed to inquire into and report upon the working of the Fisheries Act, viz.:—Messrs. O'Sullivan, Thompson, Howes, William Stephen, Stevenson, Ritchie, Nobbs, Seaver, Carruthers, and the mover, Mr. Farnell. The Committee held twenty-two meetings, examined many witnesses, including the Commissioners and several of the officers of the Fisheries Department, and took very voluminous evidence. On the 27th August, 1889, the Committee had completed its Report. It found that the Act had not worked satisfactorily, it had operated harshly upon those engaged in the industry, and had not held out sufficient encouragement to oyster-culture, which industry had indeed become almost a dead letter owing particularly to the systems of leasing and supervision being defective. The Report suggested the expediency of allowing an extension of the length of various nets, expressed regret that more discrimination had not been shown in opening and closing waters for fishing, urged attention to the way in which fish in the Murray River and its tributaries were being destroyed, recommended that encouragement be offered to persons to institute trawling, pointed out the deplorable condition of the oyster-fisheries, as well as the unsatisfactory state of affairs existing in regard to the sale of fish at the Woolloomooloo Fish Markets, urged the abolition of the Fisheries Commission and the re-establishment of the department under direct Ministerial control, or the addition of two representatives of the fishermen to the Board. The Committee concluded its Report by suggesting a consideration of the evidence submitted with it, and of two draft Bills appended thereto, which it was thought would prove of great value in settling the important questions at issue. Up to the present the labours of this Select Committee have been barren of result; the matter has several times been brought up in Parliament and discussed, but no definite legislation has been achieved; either a change of Ministry, or the consideration of measures deemed to be of greater importance, have always come in the way, and hindered the enactment of amended laws for the fisheries, which are therefore still being worked under enactments, the lines of which were, for the most part, determined so far back as 1881. The Fisheries Commissioners, also alive to the necessity for amended legislation, appended to their report for 1890 a Bill to regulate the Fisheries and Oyster Fisheries of the Colony, which had been prepared for their consideration by the Chief Inspector of Fisheries. In submitting the Bill to the Colonial Secretary, the Commissioners claimed that it avoided all the difficulties and incongruities which, in their administration of the existing law, they had found to exist. In the Bill larger power is taken for making regulations to suit circumstances as they arise, also to lease tidal waters for fishing purposes; and in respect to net and line fisheries, it proposes many provisions which experience has shown to be necessary. It then proceeds to the regulation of the oyster fisheries on entirely new lines; this part of it, however, will be specially referred to in the chapter relating to that subject. It is not known whether consideration has been given by the Government to this Bill; but until it or some kindred measure shall have been passed into law, it is hopeless to expect that the fisheries can possibly attain that importance and prominence which the natural conditions surrounding them would seem to make possible.

CHAPTER IV.

THE FISH MARKETS AND THE FISH TRADE.

THE following outline of the early history of the fish trade in this Colony is collected from information supplied by Mr. Richard Seymour, the superintendent and salesmen at the Fish Market, Woolloomooloo.

Fish began to be an article of commerce in Sydney about the year 1827. The projector of the industry was Mr. J. Lord, who, through an agent named Boyle, held sales on the race-course, now known as Hyde Park. The place of sale was subsequently removed to a house in Elizabeth-street between Goulburn and Campbell Streets. Later on again it was transferred to the Market Wharf, and afterwards to the foot of Erskine-street. At this period the supply of fish from Botany was even greater than obtains at the present time, more than 400 baskets arriving daily. This increased supply of fish afforded opportunity to others to enter the field, and Mr. Lord began to find the monopoly of the business he had so far possessed contested by persons who were eventually successful in establishing sales at the several places named, and also at the Circular Quay. In the year 1865 a further sales depôt was established in Dowling-street, Woolloomooloo. But the condition in which the fish were presented for sale, and the manner in which the sales were conducted, were beginning to create such a large amount of discontent that the Sydney Municipal Council, at the instance of the mayor at the time, Mr. Alderman John Woods, took into consideration the desirableness of attempting its regulation. The duty of instituting inquiry into the state of matters was entrusted to a civic officer, Mr. Richard Seymour. Mr. Seymour found that the discontent which had been manifested was fully justified. He reported that the modes of disposing of the fish at the several sale centres were filthy and most objectionable. The agents who had been reaping golden harvests had so far made no attempt whatever to find accommodation either for the fish brought for sale, or shelter for the women who, for the most part, were employed to convey the fish from Botany and other fishing-stations, and that, as a consequence, they had, during the early morning hours, to

The Exterior of the Fish Market.

stand exposed in all weathers, while the sales were being effected. Mr. Seymour strongly urged the establishment of a suitable fish market; but for no less a period than seven years he pressed his point in vain; however, continued representation at last began to show signs of fruitfulness, for Alderman Palmer and some others, took the matter up, with the result that in the year 1871 Mr. Michael Chapman, being mayor, the erection, at a cost of £3,000, of a market in Forbes-street, Woolloomooloo, became an accomplished fact. This first effort to place the fish trade on a recognised footing was a decided success, and so large was the increase in the amount of business transacted, that the building soon proved too small for its purpose. The City Council therefore designed and carried out additions at a further cost of £4,000. A still further increase in the fish traffic necessitated a second extension to the market, at a cost of £2,200. This addition was completed during the mayoralty of Mr. Alderman John Harris, who formally opened the enlarged building, which covers an area of over 17,000 square feet, on the 24th January, 1889.

From the time of the establishment of the fish market to the close of the year 1891, the amount realised from the sales of fish within it was £470,258 16s. 8d. The income derived during the same period, in the shape of commission on sales, rent of stalls, cleansing troughs, &c., including the cost of the building, was £20,623 0s. 1d., the result being a credit balance to the Council of £10,036 12s. 2d.

The market is open for the sale of fish for six days in each week throughout the year. The sales are effected by public auction, three staff officers holding auctioneers' licenses, performing that duty. The sales commence at 5 o'clock in the morning, and are continued until half-past 7 or 8 o'clock. The fish are parcelled in lots somewhat as follows:—Schnapper, teraglin, and nannaguy, in half-dozens, whiting, in two dozens, very large jew-fish singly, small jew-fish in half-dozens, sea-mullet in single dozens, live prawns in half-pecks, and all other fish in half-bushels. Troughs for scaling and cleaning are fixed along the whole length, and on each side of the building, and into them clean salt water is regularly pumped from the strong tide-way of the harbour off Mrs. Macquarie's Chair. The market is also furnished with a small refrigerating chamber which has done good service, but in connection with a still further extension of the building, which the Municipal Council is now undertaking, a chamber will be provided of sufficiently ample dimensions to meet any probable demand for cold storage accommodation which is likely to arise for a considerable time future. The total length of this intended addition is 113 feet 6 inches, with a breadth of the full width of the present market; of this length 46 feet will be added to the sales area, and sixteen slate cleaning troughs of a pattern similar to those already in use will be disposed along it.

The new refrigerating chambers will each measure 39 feet 9 inches by 28 feet, will occupy nearly the whole width of the market and provide a total floor space of 2,226 square feet. The eastern end of the new extension will be two storeys in height, the ground floor will be occupied by the furnaces, boilers, machinery, and other refrigerating accessories; the first floor will be subdivided into offices, storerooms, and otherwise as required. This end of the building will be surmounted by a tower about 78 feet in height in which a clock with a dial of 5 feet in diameter will be fixed. The total cost of the extension including refrigerating plant is estimated at about £6,900.

The scene at the market, during the sales, in the early morning, is a very lively one. Some idea of it may be formed from the accompanying view of its interior, taken by photography with the aid of the electric light during the progress of a morning sale. The view encompasses only a small section of the market, but it is sufficiently vivid to assist the observer in imagining the whole picture. The nature of the business transacted and the general appearance of the fish folk in market assembled has been so graphically described in the *Sydney Morning Herald*, by a contributor writing under the *nom de plume* of "Viator," that the opportunity of reproducing extracts from his contribution is gladly availed of:—

A MORNING AT THE FISH MARKETS.

By Viator.

The early pedestrian, whose inclination, want of sleep, or some other cause drives from his comfortable bed at the early hour of half-past four in the morning, may see, if his footsteps lead that way, a curious crowd assembling at the Fish Market in Woolloomooloo. There, just at the time when the ordinary sleeper unconsciously rolls over to fall into his deepest sleep, ere yet the chanticleer has begun to send forth his clarion challenge to the dawn, the traffic in fish is going on with undeniable vigour. Languid-looking Italians, swarthy Greeks, sharp Jews, and dilapidated Caucasians all gather to the sale.

The Interior of the Fish Market.

The roads outside the market are lined with vehicles of various kinds, in which the hawkers convey the fish they have purchased in the morning throughout the city. Other vehicles are arriving every now and then from the wharfs, with the harvests which have been gleaned by fishermen in various places up and down the coast. Inside, the market is scrupulously clean, and lighted with numerous lamps. When I wended my way thither, before the sun had risen yesterday morning, the air was thick with a heavy dark fog, which clung to the earth like a wet blanket. Through it the lamps in the silent deserted streets glimmered dimly like points of light, and shed their ineffectual lustre but a few feet around. In sudden contrast to the deserted streets, however, all was bustle and business at the markets. Precisely at 5 a.m. the sale began.

It may not be generally known that the fish are sold to the hawkers, or whoever chooses to purchase them by auction, and that the duty of auctioneer falls to the lot of Mr. Seymour. At 5 o'clock every morning he commences the auction, which sometimes lasts till 9 a.m. Of course, if there are any fish unfit for human food brought into the market, they are promptly seized by the inspector, and placed beyond the reach of doing any harm — a circumstance which every reader of the newspapers knows is of no infrequent occurrence. Perhaps it was the necessity of having some such inspection of the fish offered for sale to the public which induced the Corporation to place the functions of auctioneer in Mr. Seymour's hands. In any case, the conclusion the spectator of the proceedings at the Fish Markets will come to is, it could scarcely have been placed in better hands. Such a heterogeneous assemblage as that at the markets every morning, it is perhaps needless to say, even to the most casual observer of human nature, is possessed of divers idiosyncracies. Mr. Seymour is *en rapport* with them all. Every hawker is marked out, and his characteristics are evidently always before the eyes of the energetic auctioneer. Some of the buyers were clearly of an evasive turn, and these were accorded no sort of privilege by the inspector. The prompt "Come now, cash up!" of Mr. Seymour always followed a transaction with these characters, whose financial standing was perhaps of a doubtful description. Other bidders were evidently given a certain amount of credit. For some of the hawkers the auctioneer had characteristic names, such as "Nebuchadnezzar," "Ice Cream," "Dundreary," "Longbags," "Wideawake," "Grenadier," "The Soudan," "Mephistopheles," "Ivo Bligh," "Blueskin," "Graball"—an honest tradesman, with hands of more than ample description, whose tendency may perhaps be conjectured by his name; "Chips," "Daftie," and many others, all applied and accepted with equal gravity. Probably these names were fastened upon those who bear them in a jocular moment by the inspector, who is evidently the possessor of a rough mother-wit, for the exercise of which he finds time even amid the exactions of the auction. After a hurried run of prices it is somewhat humorous to hear the auctioneer exclaim "Sic, sic, sic, sic, sic, sic, (six and six), "Nebuchadnezzar," and perceive an individual with a decided facial prominence gravely step forward, and begin to shovel his fish into his basket with hands that certainly never could have been like those of his kingly namesake. For the better understanding of the scene at the markets, it is necessary to explain a little. The fish caught at Port Stephens, Lake Macquarie, Broken Bay, Port Hacking, Botany, in the harbour, and other grounds are sent by the fishermen who capture them to the agents. Of these there are five. To each agent a certain portion of the market-floor is allotted, which is enclosed by a red-line boundary. Within this again are drawn white chalk boundaries, enclosing the particular catch of each fisherman. These catches are divided into heaps,

and these heaps are disposed of *seriatim* by Mr. Seymour and his excellent assistants. The buyers have strict injunctions to stop outside the red-line, and if they step beyond it are met by the mingled ire and satire of the salesman. It takes a lot of ire and satire, however, to pierce the hides of their habitués at the fish markets, and the sale is constantly interrupted by the wild incursions into the forbidden space, and the consequent angry objurgations of the presiding genius. Driven back again and again, once more they fill the breach ; Jew face, Greek face, Italian face, and Caucasian face, eagerly and intently bent on the heaps before them, from which the dead fish turn up ghastly eyes as though reproachful of such uncalled for zeal. Some of the bidders had their hands upon their knees and their mouths open, bidding away with a ferocious frenzy, not visible in buyers in any other kind of business. Scarcely a single one of those present wore a coat ; some even disdained a vest ; while all of them had that peculiar contempt for neck gear which certain American citizens once evinced at the appearance upon a comrade of what he irefully designated a " biled shirt." And this, although the morning was cold and dark, with a bitter bite in the atmosphere suggestive of chills, and aches and rheumatism. In fact here one may find that curious class of people which is represented in every large city, who never wear coats, for it is safe to assume that a man who could go without a coat on such a morning must have a constitutional objection to coats altogether, and doubtless regards every kind of sartorial adornment as a blunder, which shows that this class has philosophically progressed farther than, or not so far as, the ordinary civilised man. The auctioneer seemed to have a well-founded distrust of some personages in the crowd, who, while not bidding for any fish, kept very close to certain outlying heaps. These were repelled by occasional sharp reminders to the effect that the auctioneer had his eye upon them, for which piece of information these characters showed becoming gratitude. Behind the grand army of hawkers, and acting as a sort of camp followers to them, were a number of ragged sharp-looking boys. As the main body pressed forward these followed on close behind, and I was assured by one of the officials that it was their habit to stoop behind the bidders at the auction and deftly rake away certain fish from between their legs. These marauders are the hardest to watch, on account of their small size and singular deftness in their profession. Withered, yellow, ragged waifs, they are like " Joe," or the " Artful," and in their own line probably quite as dexterous as the latter cool young gentleman. They are probably so prevalent at the markets in some measure because the inspector and his assistants are clad merely in civilian costume. There is nothing like the policeman's majestic uniform to strike panic into the juvenile heart inclined to err, and although through the morning a few tall policemen were looking stolidly on at the proceedings, it is yet no part of their duty to attend the sales, a circumstance which, for the sake of the small boys before mentioned, it might perhaps be as well to remedy. The auctioneer is assisted by a sturdy clerk, whose efforts, other than his clerical ones, are of considerable assistance in keeping the motley assemblage in order, and there are, besides an assistant auctioneer and clerk engaged in disposing of the fish . . . .
Ranged round the walls on either side are a succession of troughs of stone, with sea-water laid on. These are let to hawkers and fishmongers at the small sum of 5s. weekly, and in them is carried on the work of cleansing and preparing the fish for cooking. As soon as a hawker purchases his lot of fish he transports it to these troughs, and in an incredibly short space of time has it cleansed. This process is going on simultaneously with the auction, and forms a sort of accompaniment to the hurried scalings of the

auctioneer's voice. Everything necessary for cleansing purposes is placed in connection with these troughs, and those who rent them have only one fault to find with the arrangement—that is the 5s. required of them as rent. Complete arrangements are present for flushing the floors with salt water; and if this should fail through any fault in the machinery, fresh water can be obtained at a moment's notice. The old market is scarcely half the size of the new one. It is now closed awaiting demolition, as its site is to be occupied by an extension of the new market. Older still is the first fish market, now long disused. A well-known genial alderman and ex-mayor makes it a duty every morning to pay a visit to the Fish Market. In sun and rain alike he is present at the morning sales, and doubtless knows the frequenters of the place as well as the auctioneer himself. He has some interesting reminiscences to tell of the old days at the markets. "In that corner," he said, pointing to the spot, "was sold the first lot of fish ever put up in the market. The fishermen thought they could not get a sufficient price for their goods by auction, and refused to patronise the markets. One morning a fisherman put his stock in the markets by way of experiment, and was surprised to find that he received better prices for it than, if he disposed of it himself. The next day the market was full of fish, and so the auction sales were established. This market was not a good one, however, for there was something in the cement on the floor which turned the fish bad, so it had to be abandoned." The refrigerating-room in the markets is quite a modern innovation. It is situated in a corner of the old market, and is well patronised. Here may be stored any fish for which there is no sale on one morning, to be brought out fresh on the next. I saw a number of various kinds of fish disposed about it, among which were a large quantity of corpulent Murray River cod. These were afterwards put up for auction, and despite the fact that they averaged something like 14 lb. each, only realised 6s. 6d. a piece. "I don't know how it is," said Mr. Seymour, emphatically, "but our people don't like frozen fish." Considering that the fishmongers may easily obtain 1s. a pound for these fish, it is rather curious that they brought so little. Probably there is some truth in what Mr. Seymour said regarding the prejudice against frozen fish. Others besides those in the fish trade evidently utilise this refrigerating-room, as some poultry was visible hanging in a rueful fashion, head downwards from the roof. One halfpenny a pound is the charge for placing meat or fish in this room, which considering its advantages is certainly a very moderate charge.

In London and other large towns there is a market at which fish may be bought retail, and inquiries have often been made as to the reason no such place is in existence here. The answer is that it was tried, and failed. In the old market may yet be seen the stalls which were fitted up for the purpose, and rented to fishmongers. The public, owing probably to the inconvenience of the position for such a market, refused to visit it, and the enterprise lapsed; but there is no reason to suppose that such a market, placed in a central position, would not be remuneratively patronised. Although the supply of fish from Newcastle had not arrived at the market up to the time I left, owing to the delay of the steamer by the dense fog, there was a goodly supply of fish on the floor. To enumerate them all would, perhaps, not be feasible in the space allotted to me. Schnapper there were in fair quantities, and of good edible size, tinted like the mother-of-pearl shell, and beautifully fresh. The whiting—sand-whiting—were of large size, and in the pink of condition. This most delicate of breakfast fish was in great demand, and brought a substantial price. The garfish were not so

D

abundant, and somewhat small. Plenty of black bream were visible, and some were actually brought into the market alive, with their gills and fins absolutely moving. Mullet, too, were plentiful, from the harbours and lakes—not sea mullet, though, for these are only known here during some six weeks of the year. Then the market is overstocked. The clerk at the markets informed me that when they were most plentiful as many as fifteen cartloads had been sent away for manure, there being a glut in the market. What a glorious opportunity for a fish-preserving industry is lost here, and what a satire is this statement upon the enterprise of a community such as this? *In New Zealand this mullet is canned, and, to my taste—not perhaps wholly uncultured in such matters—is superior to the celebrated salmon from the Columbia and Frazer Rivers.* Some day, probably, a couple of smart Americans will take this industry in hand, and from behind their profits laugh at the apathy of this community. Whoever does it, however, will deserve their profits, for at present it is a noble gift of the Creator flouted and disdained. Of blackfish there was a large supply in the markets, but these are a cheap and poor table fish. A few—very few—soles and flounders were there, and several green eels; these latter not by any means bad eating. Some very big jewfish were sold; one fellow scaling something like 30lb. There were also a few nannygai, the handsomest of our fishes, large-eyed, and beautifully pink. A fair supply of prawns were disposed of, but no oysters, very few of which, indeed, pass through the markets. A great many complaints are made from time to time concerning the cost of fish to the public. A list of what some species brought on Friday morning will give the reader a fair idea of the profit made by the hawkers, which is certainly not enough to account for the costliness of fish to the consumer. Schnapper brought from 8s. to 12s. a dozen; squire, from 3s. to 7s.; flathead, from 3s. to 21s; whiting, from 2s. to 9s.; flounders, from 3s. to 13s.; soles, from 2s. to 5s.; jewfish, from 12s. to 72s.; mullet, from 2s. to 4s.; and eels, from 6s. to 18s. Baskets of bream, from 80 to 90 lb., brought from 10s. to 34s.; and the same weight of garfish was sold from 11s. to 18s., and of blackfish 8s. to 22s. Doubtless, the hawkers and fishmongers make a considerable profit on these prices, but then the one has to pay rent, and the other, in most cases, to support the cost of a horse and cart, as well as providing for themselves and their families.

The remedy for this is palpable. Fish must be cheapened to the hawker before it is cheapened to the public. How this may be done has frequently before been pointed out. There is fortunately no scarcity of fish in our seas, but the means of reaping the harvest of our teeming waters are unusually inadequate. In the first place, to obtain a large supply of fish it is necessary that fishermen should go further afield, and to ensure their own safety, and provide for the arrival of their fish at the Woolloomooloo markets in prime condition, they must abandon their primitive fishing-boats and take to serviceable steamers, fitted with wells or ice-rooms. At present, from the price which the fishermen's goods bring in the markets, 5 per cent. is deducted by the City Council, and the same amount is charged by the fishermen's agents. The first charge cannot reasonably be avoided by fishermen, inasmuch as they have the advantages of the market and the services of the officials for whom the Corporation pays. With reference to the second, the remedy, as an article in the *Herald* pointed out some little time ago, is in the hands of the fishermen themselves. That the gains of a fisherman even under the present system need not necessarily be small may be guessed from the facts communicated to me by a reliable authority that two fishermen at Botany sometimes shared between them as much as £800, the outcome of a single year's labour on the fruitful beaches of Botany Bay. The amount received from the markets last year by the City Council was something over £2,000.

Such is a slight sketch of our fish supply and its surroundings. Anyone wishing to obtain a glimpse at an animated scene in the quiet hours of the morning, and obtain also, together with some practical information as to the cost of fish, some new and curious impressions of human nature seen by a sidelight, will be gratified by a visit to the fish market in the early dawn of day, and when he comes away will meet the busy hawkers in every street rending the air with singular variations of a single cry, and on arriving at his own door will probably find some enterprising individual of the species endeavouring to palm off black fish for black bream, of which little trick let all good housewives beware.

A glance at the view given of the interior section of the Eastern Fish Market will show the system of parcelling the fish for sale on the floor of the market, so often complained of and so adversely criticised in the report of the Select Committee of the Legislative Assembly appointed in May, 1889, to inquire into the working of the Fisheries Act.

The chief objection taken to this arrangement is that there is no barrier to separate the public from the fish, which are frequently spat upon and trodden under foot by the crowd of larrikins and other persons who, moved either by business, curiosity, or mischief, frequent the market during the early morning sales.

The grievance, though at times ventilated in the public press, does not so far seem to have attracted the attention of the civic rulers, for the practice still continues. That fish intended for human food should be open to the possibility of such objectionable treatment does in itself seem remarkable, more especially when the evil is so easily capable of remedy.

In a recently started fish market at Redfern, abutting on the line of railway, the fish are disposed on raised tables; this method appears to answer its purpose well: the fish are preserved from possibility of damage and the buyers have larger facilities for inspecting the lots they are purchasing. Even this system is capable of improvement, and the hope may be indulged that in determining details of the proposed extension to the Eastern Market the matter may have the consideration it certainly deserves.

CHAPTER V.

THE OYSTER FISHERIES AND THE LAWS REGULATING THEM.

It will be assumed that the perusal of the chapter on the fishing-grounds has supplied the reader with a sufficient knowledge of the geography of the coast of New South Wales to enable him, by the aid of an occasional reference to the coastal map which accompanies this pamphlet, to apprehend the position of the several waters which, in the present connection, will engage his attention.

So far as the oyster fisheries are concerned the classification of the coastal-line into three divisions will for the sake of convenience be disregarded. Oysters can be maintained out of water in marketable condition for such a length of time that supplies drawn from the remotest coastal waters may be utilised for food with almost as much facility as those taken from places quite adjacent to the metropolis. Hence the whole coast can be placed under contribution, and for the growth and culture of the oyster there is no part of the world better adapted. The climate, the nature of the coast-line with its innumerable inlets and creeks, and the natural existence in several varieties of the bivalve itself all combine to mark its suitability for successful ostreiculture. Unlike the coasts of England and Scotland, where the temperature in the summer months is often sufficient to prevent the shedding of spat at all, and nearly always to limit the quantity of it—here we have invariably the spat distributed in almost unlimited profusion. And yet, notwithstanding these unusual advantages, the fact has to be admitted that at the present time the beds and deposits are not yielding a sufficient supply even for our own consumption. Time was, and not very long ago either, when that supply was more than sufficient to satisfy the Victorian markets in addition to those of New South Wales. The causes which led to the existing serious decrease can be traced, and to a considerable extent they are, fortunately, capable of removal, or at least of abatement. Imperfect legislation has been a principal, though not the sole factor. About it something will be said further on. Natural causes, and nature works on a large scale, have been at work too on lines inimical to ostreal development; that development is, to a great extent, dependent on the proportion of salt held in the water in which the oyster occurs; if that proportion be materially exceeded or decreased the food producing conditions will be disturbed, development will be retarded, and the oyster will cease to grow, or perhaps die right out.

Now, during several years past, New South Wales has been experiencing a succession of droughts more or less severe, and during the same period her oyster-beds have been suffering depletion to such an extent that while in 1883 they yielded the comparatively large supply of 46,377 bushels, in the present year, 1891, they have produced only 14,181 bushels. Now, a connection is to be easily traced between these periods of drought and oyster depletion. Oysters on our seaboard occur under two distinct features of location, viz., on beds in depths of water ranging to six or more fathoms (popularly known as deep-water beds), and on the shore between low and high water mark (distinguished as foreshore deposits).

The deep-water beds have always held a special value by reason of the superiority of their produce over that of the foreshores. Now, fresh water being a condition essential to the growth of the oyster, the question arises, how can it with its lesser specific gravity reach these deep beds. It is obvious that it must reach them by some other means than from the surface, and the readiest solution is that it is conveyed from the surrounding country by subterranean courses along and under the floors of rivers and inlets, and wherever it meets with porous soil it wells up, and mingling with the salt water creates one of the conditions necessary to oyster growth; and in such places the spat, which, as has been stated, is distributed in lavish profusion, falls, and a deep-water bed is formed. With the progress of the droughts this supply of fresh water would begin to fail, and with it the food supply, and eventually ceasing to flow at all, the oyster, as a consequence, would have to succumb and give place to forms of marine life and vegetation, which could not previously exist. This theory was in part practically illustrated at the Clarence River, in one of the estuaries, in which sponge and other submarine growth had completely overcome an oyster-bed. A flood subsequently occurring and the estuary being shallow, the water coming down in large volume affected the bottom, destroying and clearing away all the obstructive growth, and to-day on that same area exists one of the most prolific beds which the Colony possesses.

It is easy thus to account for the fact of the deep-water beds having ceased their yield—the lower water had become too salt to sustain oyster life—the sources of supply were thus reduced to the foreshore deposits, the top water therein still maintaining a sufficient percentage of saltness. The correctness of this theory, which the writer, about ten years since, had officially promulgated, has been practically demonstrated by Mr. Henry Woodward, the lessee of some extensive oyster fisheries, who has devoted much time to the study and practice of ostreiculture. In an interesting brochure which he has written, he describes an experiment he had instituted for increasing the productive capabilities of some of his beds at Wallis' Lake; he got satisfactory results, but at the time he never dreamt of attributing it to the salinity of the water :—

About four years ago (he writes), I leased the oyster-beds at Wallis' Lake. The oysters had become very scarce, but my men told me there was an immense quantity of oysters on a bank, which, if laid down on the beds, would grow into good oysters.

I went there, and this is a description of the place : You enter the Heads and are at once in the lake, which is studded with islands. Oysters begin to show from the very entrance, but run small, as they do at most places near the sea. The good part of the fishery begins at about two miles from the entrance from the sea and extends about two miles up. About three miles from the entrance is the mouth of the River Wollomba, which empties itself in the lake. Now, at the mouth of this river a great bank of sand, shells, &c., runs right across, which blocks the salt water from running up and the fresh from running down, except at the top of high water.

It was on the top of this bank the great quantity of oysters laid, but, owing to the short time water covered them, they grew very slowly and were always poor in quality. These were the oysters I now began to operate on, by removing them off the high bank and placing them in beds upon which they would always be in water. I had one portion of them carried up the river, and laid upon an old bed situated well out in the river, and over which there was always from 9 in. to 15 in. of water ; the remainder were carried down into the lake and laid on a bed that had been a famous one for breeding and fattening purposes.

In about six months' time the result began to show. The oysters that had been laid up the river grew into first-class oysters ; those that had been laid in the lake died. Six thousand bushels of oysters were laid on that lakebed, and they were literally all lost. I could name the whole of the men that were engaged in the work. They are all at work on our rivers; many of them work for me at the present time.

Not one of us engaged in this work could at that time give any feasible reason why one portion of the oysters laid down had all died and the others did well, for at that time we never thought of salt as a factor in the matter ;

but now how easy to account for the loss of one portion and the improvement of the other. Those oysters laid up the river had water suitable to their life, owing to the fresh water flowing on top of the salt, and they lying so near to the top of the tide ; and those oysters laid down on the lake-bed died because the water they were put in was too salt, being very little different from the pure salt water of the ocean. Here is a remarkable proof, that the life and propagation of the oyster is entirely dependent on the salinity of the water.

But not only by drought has nature been warring against oyster life, she has been assailing it also through the agency of a small marine worm (*polydora ciliatus*); this worm has proved a source of great trouble wherever it has made its appearance, and unfortunately it has found its way, more or less, into the principal oyster-bearing waters. The Hunter River has been most severely affected, and has cost the lessee of the larger beds there, Mr. F. J. Gibbins, no end of labour and expense. There are now signs of improvement in many of the beds, and there is reason for hope that the eradication of this pest may, at no distant date, be accomplished. It was at one time supposed, from appearances, that this worm effected its entrance to the oyster by boring through the shell, but a scientific inquiry into the whole matter which, at the instance of the Commissioners of Fisheries, was instituted, soon disposed of the boring theory as being out of the question. This inquiry, which was undertaken by Mr. Thomas Whitelegge, F.R.M.S., a zoologist attached to the staff of the Australian Museum, shows that the young worm simply swims into the open oyster and fixes itself by its head on the margin of the shell, where it immediately begins to construct a tube and collect a large quantity of mud, and this it seems capable of doing in a very short time. The mud is immediately covered over by the oyster with a thin layer of nacre, and the worm is imprisoned with its mud in a very small space. Should the oyster be out of condition, or should it have suffered from previous visits of the worm, the nacre is deposited more slowly, and the efforts of the worm gaining the ascendancy, the oyster gradually succumbs and dies. Extracts from Mr. Whitelegge's report, which is very instructive and interesting, and is written in familiar language, will be found amongst the appendices to this pamphlet. Man too, as well as the drought and the worm, has materially assisted in effecting the destruction of the oyster deposits, for, availing of defects which have revealed themselves in the Oyster Fisheries Act, unprincipled persons set themselves out to rob large extents of unleased foreshores in every inlet and river of all the oysters they contained, leaving hundreds of miles bare of a single live shell, and whenever practicable they turned their attention to areas under lease also, and cleared them of oysters in like manner. When the Act was first passed it was quite the fashion for persons to acquire a lease of shore for oyster-culture. The majority of these persons knew not anything, nor, indeed, professed to know anything, of the science of culture, and moreover, being often resident in places remote from their holdings, they had not proper control of the oysters which were growing naturally upon them. The result was that all who chose could gather them with but little risk of detection. How well these pilferers availed themselves of the opportunity thus afforded is made apparent by the denuded state in which the beds and deposits appear to-day. With three or four exceptions, culture in the true sense of the term has not been practised at all, so that—owing to droughts, the ravages of the worm, defective legislation, and the still greater enemy, man himself—the impoverished state of our beds and deposits is not to be wondered at. The most prolific beds, under the most favourable oyster-producing conditions, could not have withstood the wreckage to which the New South Wales deposits have been subjected. There is the startling fact, collected from official records, that while in the year 1876 not less than 93,000 bushels of oysters which helped to supply the Victorian as well as our own markets, were produced from the New South Wales beds, the total quantity which could be gathered in 1891 was but 14,181 bushels, and for some time past New South Wales has been receiving much of her supply from outside sources.

A remedy for this, in the shape of improved legislation based on a more extended knowledge of requirements than was available previously, is to hand; the worm pest is disappearing; land hitherto parched and thirsty has been refreshed by copious rains; and accounts are being received of immense falls of spat and plenteous crops of brood and ware.

Accepting these as indications of the dawn of improved prospects there seems ample warrant for anticipating that in the immediate future the oyster-beds will not only have assumed their original productiveness, but perhaps, under wise legislative restriction and encouragement, will have so far exceeded it that, in addition to the supply to repletion of the most extravagant demand for home need, the establishment of a large export trade will be possible.

Now, these expectations have reference only to the oyster deposits in the coastal rivers and inlets; while in addition to these there are assumed to exist in the deep sea itself beds which have not even been searched for, and which consequently have not suffered spoliation at the hands of man. The evidence of the existence of such beds seems indisputable. On portions of the coast quite remote from inlet of any kind are to be found immature oysters in quantity cultched to the rocks. These must have their origin somewhere in the ocean depths. Of course they do not thrive on these wave-beaten rocks. They simply exist; the salinity of the water and the turbulence of the sea are not conditions favourable to their development. The same may be said of the oysters literally plastered sometimes a foot or more in thickness on the rocks just inside harbours and inlets, such, for instance, as Port Hacking. They ever remain diminutive, and worthless as an article for consumption. As has already been advanced in respect to the occurrence of oyster-beds in rivers and inlets, so in the deep sea also, there must be places where the fresh water oozes up from under the ocean floor, and meeting suitable bottom produces the food and other conditions necessary to oyster growth and development. Else, if it were not so, how is the presence of oysters in lake channels to be accounted for? Instance, for example, Lake Macquarie or Lake Illawarra. In neither of those waters are oysters to be found, and oysters placed therein for experiment have died. Surely, the reason they died was because, as a converse to the position taken in regard to sea water, these lake waters had not a sufficient salinity to sustain oyster life. Therefore, if oysters occurring, as they do occur, in these lake channels, are not the produce of oysters in the lakes themselves, and if oysters are found on the sea rocks in places quite remote from rivers or inlets of any kind, where can they have had their origin if not from the floor of the deep sea itself?

Lakes Macquarie and Illawarra have been instanced, in support of this contention, as being waters the conditions of which are more generally known; but the same argument will apply to every coastal inlet. Off the Clarence River Heads an oyster-bed was once discovered, but its position has been lost. About four miles north-east from the Hunter River there are on the shore evidences of the existence of an oyster-bed. At Catherine Hill Bay, an indentation of the coast open to the sea, and near to which no inlet of any kind exists, similar evidences are present. The same occurrence is to be traced off the Crookhaven River, and off nearly every lake and river in the more southern districts of Pambula and Eden. Indeed, off Merimbula an impromptu dredging experiment, undertaken by Mr. F. W. Smithers, the travelling inspector of fisheries, revealed the actual existence of oysters on the sea bottom; had the experiment been followed up, there was every reason for expecting most successful results. Is there not then ample warrant for assuming that really untold wealth is waiting only to be gathered—that it extends along the whole length of the coastal line, and needs only development to become an important factor in the supply of this nutritious food?

THE OYSTER FISHERIES LAWS.

Until the year 1866 no thought seems to have been bestowed upon the economic value of the oyster. So far from any attempt to foster it for food purposes, this mollusc was regarded merely as a superior material for the lime-kiln. Other non-edible shell-fish existed in profusion, but lime from the live oyster had an especial value and always a large demand, and secured a high price; consequently, oyster deposits were placed under contribution to satisfy large contracts. One contract is noted for the supply of 6,000 bushels of lime from the shells of live oysters. To any casual observer the criminality of this shameful waste ought to have been abundantly obvious; and yet when, in the year named, Dr. John Bowie Wilson, in his place in Parliament, directed attention to the matter, there were to be found legislators who disputed the necessity for legislation to check the abuse, and to brand as absurd his proposal to enact a law to establish a property in oysters. About the end of 1867, Dr. Wilson renewed the matter with more success—his efforts, in conjunction with those of Mr. James Squire Farnell, also a member of the Legislature, were the means of obtaining an Act of Parliament, intituled the "Oyster Fisheries Act, 1868." Its objects were the prevention of the exhaustion and threatened extinction of the oyster-beds, the formation and cultivation of artificial beds, and the improvement of the natural beds. Burning live oysters for lime was absolutely prohibited, and the leasing of areas for propagation encouraged. This Act, purely an experimental measure, and which was passed in the face of strong opposition, did good work in its season; it brought the oyster fisheries under partial official control, vastly increased the supply, and secured a substantial revenue. In time, however, difficulties arose as to the respective rights of lessees and licensed dredgers; the Act failed to meet the growing requirements, and its administration became hopelessly confused. In a very interesting address delivered before the Linnean Society of New South Wales, Doctor James C. Cox, F.L.S., the President thereof, and at the time the President of the Fisheries Commission also, fully describes the misworking of this Act, and the causes which led to the confusion. Dr. Cox's paper will be found in the Appendix. Repeated representations of the irregularities which Dr. Cox thus recorded had previously resulted in the appointment, in the year 1876, of a Royal Commission on Oyster-culture, consisting of the Honorable Thomas Holt, a member of the Legislative Council, the Honorable John Bowie Wilson, and James Squire Farnell, Esquire, a member of the Legislative Assembly. Each of these gentlemen had evidenced large interest in the development of this important industry, and Mr. Holt, the Chairman of the Commission, had, in addition, acquired a practical acquaintance with the subject by a minute and lengthened inspection of the methods of culture employed on the French coasts, and which methods he afterwards carried out, at an enormous outlay, on his own estates at George's River. Unfortunately Mr. Holt did not obtain any return for his expenditure; he found that the claires which he had constructed were not suitable to grow oysters in the high temperature which prevails here during the summer months. Mr. Holt's unfortunate experience may have been of great value in diverting others from experiments in culture in a similar direction.

The Commission entered very exhaustively into the subject entrusted to it, and took extensive evidence. It resulted in its recommending the cancellation of improperly issued leases of natural oyster-beds, and the substitution of a system of licensing under a royalty, the leasing of ground for artificial culture, and the registration or licensing of all persons engaged in the trade. A comprehensive Bill on these bases, and embodying other necessary regulating provisions, was appended to their Report.

Through Cabinet changes the Bill was never brought before Parliament. Mr. Farnell applied for and obtained leave to bring it up, but before he could do so the Ministry of the day had resigned office. By this misadventure, for such it certainly was so far as the subject under consideration was concerned, the injudicious working of the extensive river leases continued, with two or three exceptions, until their expiry. One lessee had a monopoly of no less than three separate rivers at one time, and enjoyed almost perfect immunity from restriction as to the size or quantity of the oysters he might take from them.

In 1880 the Royal Commission, under the presidency of the Honorable (afterwards Sir) William Macleay, elsewhere noticed at length in this pamphlet, undertook to deal with the vexed question of the oyster fisheries. The result of its labours was the enactment of Part II of the Fisheries Act, 1881, which first of all validated the existing leases which had been professedly issued under the Oyster-beds Act of 1868, and then created two separate methods by which the public might in future acquire leases of the shores and beds of tidal waters. The first of these, popularly known as the *long lease*, as it might cover the lengthened term of thirty years, with right of renewal for a similar period, allowed persons an area of 25 acres of tidal waters, but excluding natural oyster-beds, the Act having reserved those for the use of dredgers working under license. Rent was fixed at 5s. per acre per annum for the first four years, and at 20s. per acre yearly for the remainder of the term. The second was an annual lease of shore fronting alienated land, carrying right of renewal from year to year. Shore, defined by the Act to mean the portion of Crown land between mean high and mean low-water mark, could, under this form, be leased only to the owner, occupier, or lessee of the abutting land; the rental was fixed at the rate of 20s. for every 100 lineal yards of shore. An exclusive right to these frontage waters became thus created in favour of riparian owners, at the expense of the general public. The revenue generally was to be derived from the rents accruing under the leases, from a royalty on oysters dredged from natural beds, and from fees for licenses issued to dredgers and dealers. The special provision made in the previous

Acts for preventing the destruction of oysters consequent upon the conversion of the shells of the live animals into lime was maintained. A very brief practical experience of this measure proved that it was in some respects unworkable, and the assistance of the Legislature had again to be invoked to cure the difficulties which had manifested themselves. Consequently a new measure was introduced into Parliament, which eventuated in the enactment of the Oyster-beds Act of 1884. Mr. (afterwards Sir) Alexander Stuart, the head of the Government at the time, in moving the second reading, said somewhat as follows:—"The necessity for the Bill arises in this way. When the Fisheries Act of 1881 was passed the Colony had been suffering for a considerable time under a system of leasing the oyster fisheries, which turned out to be very destructive in its character, and it was necessary, as these leases were about to fall in, to pass some legislation on the subject. The late Government introduced a Bill, which was passed, and it has proved to be utterly unworkable, although no doubt it was passed with the very best intentions—that of remedying the difficulties which had grown up under former legislation. These difficulties were avoided to a considerable extent, but they were succeeded by other difficulties of another character. A number of leases to carry out the object of the Act, which was to improve the culture of oysters, as contra-distinguished from the taking up of the oysters wherever they have been naturally deposited, have been applied for. The object of the Act is to increase the culture of oysters. Applications for leases to the extent of two or three hundred to carry out oyster-culture have been made. The industry would no doubt be very beneficial to the country, but, owing to the incompleteness of the Act and certain restrictions, and other difficulties which have arisen, it has been found quite impossible to grant those leases in accordance with the intention of the law. To enable these leases to issue it has been found necessary to introduce this Bill. I need not now enter into the various provisions which are considered desirable for that purpose. It will be sufficient to state that it is intended that the same conditions shall apply to tidal waters which lie in front of private property as to tidal waters which are in front of Crown lands. It is not considered wise or desirable that persons merely because they happen to have land abutting upon water should be able to act the dog in the manger, neither taking out leases to improve the culture of oysters nor enabling others to do so. The Act of 1881 recognised a right which does not exist under any English law—the right of the owner of the abutting land to the water below low-water mark. The recognition of that right gives to these persons the liberty to prevent any one from carrying on this particular industry of oyster-cultivation below the high-water mark of the tidal waters in front of their land. We propose to abolish this right. Another restriction which rendered the issue of leases impossible was that which rendered it illegal for any lease to include a portion of a natural oyster-bed. The question arose as to what a natural oyster-bed was. Unfortunately there no longer remain any large oyster-beds. Under the operation of the Acts of 1867 and 1871 they have been entirely dredged away; but there are in various places a commencement of what may be termed re-formations of natural beds. I take it that the natural oyster-bed is a deposit of oysters placed independently of man's instrumentality. How the oysters are attracted, whether by the particular quality of the ground, or the power of the oyster in the embryonic state to place itself in localities in which particular food is to be found, we cannot say; but at all events the beds which we understand by natural beds are those which exist in contradistinction to artificially-formed beds. In most of the tidal waters suited for oyster-culture there are to some extent natural oyster-beds in process of formation. It was found impossible to issue leases in accordance with the Act, which prohibits any portion of a natural bed from being included in a lease. We propose that leases of areas may be issued, notwithstanding that they may contain a portion of a natural oyster-bed, and we give to the lessee the exclusive right of gathering the oysters on his own leasehold. As we establish a royalty on all oysters taken, it is a matter of indifference as to who actually is the cultivator of the oyster. Under the present system dredging licenses are given for natural oyster-beds. It will be seen that if a portion of a natural bed exists on a part of a leased area, the licensed dredgers would be entitled to go upon that area under his right to dredge the natural bed. This would be intolerable; there would be a constant conflict between the two parties. We have therefore abolished the system under which licenses were issued for oyster-dredging. No doubt, in order that the production of the oyster may be continued, it will be necessary to make certain reserves to secure the spatting of oysters during the season. It is necessary to produce the Bill at the present time in order that another season may not be lost, to the great detriment of the whole trade in oysters, and to the discomfort of many who are accustomed to indulge in this delicious mollusc. These are the main provisions of the Bill, and without any reference to what may be termed the secondary provisions."

This Bill, with a few unimportant modifications, became law, and, excepting a subsequent amendment, by which the royalty it imposed on oysters gathered from the beds and foreshores became abolished, it remains the law by which those fisheries are still regulated. A more lengthened experience of the working capabilities of this enactment has forced the unwelcome conclusion that even it does not contain sufficiently restrictive provisions to further the development of the large possibilities of these fisheries. It certainly checked for a time the wholesale denudation of the oyster deposits, which were being carried on by licensed dredgers, who worked them according to their own sweet will, in total disregard of any obligation to assist in maintaining a continuity of supply; but in its passage through Parliament some of its more important sections were so marred by unfortunate amendments, which seem to have passed only because the effect of them could not be apprehended, that the resulting consequences were to reduce the protective value of the measure in a very material degree. One instance may be given: The 9th section of that Act makes it penal to take oysters without authority from a reserve or a leased area, but it omits the protection of oysters on the extensive shore areas which are not under lease at all. The result has been that unprincipled persons have taken small leases of one or two hundred yards of shore for the purpose of artificial culture, and these have not only failed in performing the obligations of their leases, but, availing of the laxity of the terms in which this 9th section is couched, proceeded to rob the adjacent unleased foreshores of every shell they contained; as this practice has been followed in almost every water, the exhaustion of the fisheries need not be regarded with surprise; and the abolition of the royalty on oysters, which was effected to cure what was described as the anomaly of charging a royalty on our own oysters, while admitting free of duty oysters from other countries, offered an additional facility to these thieves, for it opened the door to participation in these robberies to any man who could manage to scrape together twenty shillings to pay for the rent of one hundred yards of shore.

Naturally these omissions have had most anxious consideration by the Board of Commissioners to whom the regulation of the fisheries generally is entrusted, and they have made several efforts to cure them, but so far without avail, for the time of the Legislature has been so over-occupied by what has been deemed more important business that legislation for the fisheries has been out of question. However, the delay will not have been all loss. The experience gained has been so large, and the knowledge of requirements so increased, that it is now possible to present to Parliament a measure so extended in its scope and complete in its details as may possibly suffice without amendment for a long future period.

Such a measure is to be found in Part 3 of the Bill for the regulation of the Fisheries and Oyster Fisheries of the Colony elsewhere noticed in this pamphlet. This part of the Bill provides for leasing Crown lands for oyster culture, and it differs in principle from the present law in so far that it takes power to lease land in large areas; it also provides for the protection of oysters on unleased Crown lands; further, assuming the existence of undiscovered oyster deposits in the open sea, it regulates the manner in which such may be worked.

Amongst other provisions, lessees are to be required to find sureties for the payment of their rent. The purpose of this is to prevent persons who have leased oyster-bearing areas from stripping them of oysters and then practically throwing the areas back on the Crown, as has been so frequently done under the present Act, and has resulted in such heavy arrears of rent, which, in many instances, it will, we fear, be impossible to recover.

The following brief description of the oyster deposits in some of the principal waters may be of interest:—

THE CLARENCE RIVER OYSTER FISHERIES.

This fishery is small, but for its size very productive. The principal beds are the Home or House Bed, under lease to A. Ross; this bed is about 600 yards in length; Brodie's bed, extending from the Home bed for about 600 yards on both sides of the portion of the River locally known as Oyster Creek. Further up this creek is the Rot-gut Bed under lease to A. Phelps.

The Clarence River oysters are not of first quality, nor do they during the summer months keep well for more than a few days after removal from the water. The shells, like the oyster in condition, are unusually soft, owing probably to some special properties in the water. The old lake-beds some two or three miles above the lower fishery have not borne oysters for many years. Formerly they produced the best that grew at the Clarence. They are similar in appearance to the Manning River oysters, and, unlike the lower beds, are of good flavour.

THE MANNING RIVER OYSTER FISHERY.

Twelve years since this fishery was one of the finest in the Colony, but subsequently, from causes unknown, it ceased to grow oysters; it is only during the last two years that it has shown signs of improvement. Oysters appear within the entrance and extend along the right-hand shore; the principal deposit is, or rather was, the Bar Bed, but the occurrence of repeated floods covered it with many feet of the sand and rubbish that are carried down a river in floodtime; although now nearly clean again oysters will neither settle on it naturally nor live if laid there. The next bed, is the Cattai, so designated from a creek of that name. Seventeen or eighteen years since it produced a splendid oyster, when, from unknown causes, like the Bar Bed it closed its supply and has not had a marketable value since. About eighteen months ago, however, a first-class crop of brood appeared which is developing into a full oyster; a profitable result therefore in the near future is expected. A similar experience belongs to McDermot's bed—after eighteen years of barrenness it now contains a large crop of young oysters which the lessee is retaining for purposes of increase—the oysters are of first quality and good in shape. Scott's Creek bed, so-called from a creek of that name, suffered in like manner until about two years since, when it became stocked, this stock being nursed in like manner to that on the Cattai Creek Bed.

Another deposit, an old shore lease, producing only bankers, is heavily stocked now, but is being left unworked with the view to future increased yield. The South Passage bed, one

E

of the most prolific in the river, like some of the others described, failed in its producing powers for several years; now it is one of the most heavily stocked. There are three other leases, in reality one bed, locally known as the Rocks; this bed is about three-quarters of a mile in length and extends in several parts right across the river. After many years of barrenness oysters made their appearance here about eighteen or twenty months since, and it now contains a heavy stock. Another bed, locally known as Latham's bed and Shoobert's Rocks, contains a splendid crop of oysters nearly fit for market. On Syron's bed oysters thrive well, are in plenty, and are of a first quality. The beds thus briefly described comprise the whole of the fishery.

From what has been written it will be gathered that the Manning River beds as a whole failed absolutely in this yield during the whole decade from 1880; the causes of the failure are unknown; as a matter of conjecture it may be attributed to the absence of the due proportion of salt in the water necessary to their existence; but the cause, whatever it may have been, is evidently removed, and with the care and the attention being bestowed by the lessees who are judiciously husbanding their stocks it may be confidently expected that this erstwhile prolific water will shortly resume its position as one of the principal of the Colony's fisheries.

WALLIS LAKE OYSTER FISHERIES.

Oysters in this lake occur immediately within the heads, but owing to the strength of the sea-water are of small size. Passing upwards to Breckenridge's Creek, which more properly might be termed a river, are to be found the foreshore oysters or bankers as they are properly termed; bankers in shape, and in quality not to be excelled; this is the only part of the fishery in which this class of oysters are produced; the two leases therein, Nos. 711 and 551, comprise all the mangrove and cobbler's pegs (mangrove roots) ground; branching from the shores are many little creeks taking their rise not far back in the land; these two leases are splendid catchment grounds for the spat from the spawning oyster; the practice adopted by the lessee, Mr. Henry Woodward, has been to remove the young brood and more or most of it higher up the lake on better growing and fattening ground, but the catchment areas become, in a few months, as thickly stocked as ever. On crossing the creek to lease No. 898, at the head of Goodwin Island, it will be found that the oysters alter both in shape and quality, being a species of half-dredge and half-banker. Passing along to lease No. 2,177 magnificent oyster-bearing shores abounding with oysters present themselves. The shores all around Cockatoo Island are perfect natural oyster-grounds, and as such are, in the opinion of the lessee, not to be excelled in any part of the world; one can start from the shore banks outwards for 100 yards or more in a depth of water not exceeding 12 or 15 inches in any part; the bottom is composed of cockle shells, as indeed is all the lake floor of this splendid fishery. Practically, the whole of it is one vast natural bed, and the covering water being both clear and shallow it is unsurpassed for purposes of observation and experiment.

The oyster in this lake is thick and cuppy as any genuine dredge oyster and its flavour is not to be surpassed. Leases No. 181, between the islands and the two leases at Clement's Bay, Nos. 1,625 and 2,055, are of similar character and produce as excellent oysters as those on the Cockatoo Island leases.

At the mouth of the Wollomba River, on the left hand side, is a broad oyster-bank extending across the water; close inshore on the left-hand side is an artificial cutting to allow of the passage of small crafts up the river; from this work the great bank upon which the oysters grow so well has been named the Cutting Bed; it is a most prolific propagating ground, its yields of oysters being simply immense; the bed is about 500 yards in length by from 100 to 300 yards in breadth. It is curious that while the shores on the left-hand side of the Wollomba River are for the most part oyster-producing, those on the right-hand side are absolutely bare.

Beyond the Cutting Bed is the Middle Flat Bed; it produces a splendid, deep, well-flavoured oyster, but is remarkable for an exceptionally hard shell. The waters in this fishery are evidently strongly impregnated with lime as may be inferred from the unusual character of the shells. Further on is the top lease, No. 1,971, the Broadwater Bed; this bed is the deepest in the fishery and develops the largest oyster; when full grown they are round, deep, and full of solid white flesh, and large as they are they possess all the delicate flavour of the smaller oyster. This bed has not of late years been contributing its quota of supply, but it is now well stocked with brood and ware.

HUNTER RIVER OYSTER FISHERIES.

Not many years since the beds in this river were amongst the most prolific in the Colony. They yielded on an average from 150 to 200 bags per week. At one time, when they were worked under license by dredgers, there were won from them no less than 2,056 bags, each containing 3 bushels, in the short space of two months. The beds principally worked were what are known as the Bay Beds. In the still earlier days, when oysters were burnt for lime, as many as 400 and 500 bags were collected weekly from these beds, the Beacon Bed and the Schnapper Beds. The Bay Beds are in water from 1 foot to 10 or 12 feet. The several beds in the bay are distinguished as the Green Shells, the Middle Bank, and the Schnapper Bed. Of these, the best is the Middle Bank. Schnapper Bed is 500 yards long by 100 yards wide, covered by about 5 feet of water. The Beacon Bed, in the main channel, is 600 yards long by 200 yards wide. It had a great repute in former years, and grew a large brown-shelled oyster. The Green Shell Bed produced a superior oyster, which always commanded a higher market price than any of the others. The Bluff Bed is about 300 yards long by 100 yards wide, and is covered by a depth of water varying from 1 foot to 20 feet. Hughes' bed, in the Back Channel, is moderately prolific. It was here that the worm first made its appearance, from whence it extended all over the river. Spawn set several times in quantity, but on each occasion it was overcome by the pest. The Back Channel Beds are now recovering, and there is a slight improvement in the Bay Beds. The succession of floods which has occurred in this river has completely smothered some of the beds with deposits of mud and rubbish.

HAWKESBURY RIVER OYSTER FISHERIES.

In this river the grounds generally seem distinctly separated into two classes—those suitable for culture and those for breeding; the former embrace the shores of the creeks and upper parts of the main river; the latter the lower parts of the main river and the mouths of the creeks. The culture or fattening grounds, as a rule, improve as they reach towards the oyster-bearing limit. The ostreal value of the waters may be classed in the following order :—Mooney, Berowra, and Marra Marra Creeks; Porto Bay, the foreshores off Milson Island, and Mullet and Mangrove Creeks. There are not any deepwater beds in the Hawkesbury River, except in Berowra Creek, but oysters taken from the shores and placed in suitable localities thrive rapidly. There is no general time for spatting—it occurs in different parts at different times. The shores of the lower main river, especially those of Dangar and Long Islands, are very prolific as breeding-grounds and spat collectors; indeed, as already stated, all the shores of the lower river are especially suitable for this purpose. At the present time the river is practically bare of oysters—its proximity to Sydney and the facilities which exist for transit to all parts of it have had their effects in keeping the shores in a denuded state; adding to this the extensive ravages of the worm, it might be concluded that culture would be next to impossible, but it is not so; the ostreal fertility of some of the creek tributaries, Mooney Creek especially, is so great that it needs only a comparatively short time of closure against oyster gathering to enable it to recuperate. The Commissioners of Fisheries, availing themselves of the very imperfect provision in this regard which the existing law enacts, are endeavouring to effect such a closure. The result will be looked forward to with interest and with hopefulness, for it is on record that in former years the ware of oysters laid in Mooney Creek developed in ten months into a full-sized marketable article.

GEORGE'S RIVER OYSTER-BEDS.

These beds, like those of the Hawkesbury, have suffered materially from the ravages of worm and man—their proximity to Sydney has rendered their denudation, that is, so far as the foreshore oysters are concerned, very easy of accomplishment; nevertheless, these likewise possess great power of recuperation and with such reservation from gathering as can be given to them the day may not be distant when the beds will have resumed their old producing powers. The first bed in this water is at Woniora Point, at the entrance to the river, the second at O'Connell's Bay, about a mile up; at this latter, in about 12 feet of water, is a natural bed—another such bed exists at Caravan Point. The oysters here are of the mud and deep-water kinds, and exist in medium quantity. At Points Neverfail and Jewfish the oysters are obtained by diving, being covered by 25 to 40 feet of water; they are excellent in quality and great in quantity. At Overreach the oysters grow in 16 feet depth of water, and in small quantities.

The next place worthy of note is the "Moon," which has a depth of 16 feet below low-water mark. The best oysters in George's River can be procured from this bed, but only by diving.

Half a mile further on is "Soily Bottom," a bed 76 feet deep below low-water mark. The oysters here do not grow plentifully; the strong ebb tide has quite a deteriorating effect.

The last place where oysters may be collected in George's River is at the mouth of Salt Pan Creek, in a depth from 10 to 12 feet. The oysters are of good quality, but not plentiful.

Woronora is a branch off George's River; in a depth of 15 feet, the deep-water rock oysters are found. This is the only spot up this branch where mud oysters can be procured.

Half a mile beyond this bed some deep-water rock oysters are found, in about 4 feet of water.

At Clarke's Point, further on, in a depth of 8 feet, they grow in abundance.

There are three sorts of oysters in George's River, namely, mud, deep-water rock, and foreshore oysters. The difference is that mud oysters are found lying on flat rocks and in the crevices; some of them may be found attached to the rocks. It is a remarkable fact that these oysters will not keep longer than fifteen hours out of water, and then must be kept in a cool place. No spawn from these oysters has ever been artificially laid in George's River—they are all of natural growth. The deep-rock oysters are twice the size of the foreshore oysters. Some idea of their dimensions may be formed when it is stated that some of them would not pass through a ring 3 inches in diameter—they are fit for food after being kept for about fifteen days. The foreshore oysters are something similar to the deep-water rock kind, but are much smaller and flatter.

There have been no oysters in the natural dredging beds for the last five or six years, except those which were artificially laid, and they came originally from Port Hacking, Wienne, and Cuggara mangroves. Of these artificially-laid oysters, 300 bags were laid in O'Connel's bed, and yielded 400 bags of remarkably fine oysters twelve months afterwards.

SHOALHAVEN AND CROOKHAVEN RIVERS OYSTER FISHERIES.

In Broughton Creek, a tributary of the Shoalhaven River, are four separate beds; the first, nearest to the entrance, is about 100 yards long by 6 yards wide. Owing to considerable deposits of silt which have occurred during the last three or four years its producing capabilities have become much impaired; the bottom which is rocky as most of the beds in this district are, is covered by a depth of 12 feet of water; the oysters on this bed are large and cuppy.

The second bed is about half a mile from the entrance and is known as Fraiser's bed; a quarter of a mile further on is the third bed, the fourth being situated nearly a mile above it; all of these were at one time heavily stocked with oysters, but they have all suffered from ravages of the worm, and are but little in repute at the present time.

In the Crookhaven River there is practically but one bed; it is called the Dock Bed; the bottom is rocky and is covered by a depth of 10 feet of water; there were other small deposits in this river, on shelly bottoms, but they are now silted up and useless.

THE CLYDE RIVER OYSTER-BEDS.

The principal oyster deposits in this river bear distinctive appellations. There is the *old bed* nearest the sea some 300 yards long by 150 yards wide, and covered by an average depth of water of 12 feet—the bottom consists of hard mud overlaid with dirt shells—spawn does not fix to it nor indeed to any of the others of its class, but brood, of which there are quantities on the adjacent shores, become, after being placed in this bed for twelve or fifteen months, a marketable commodity.

Pelican Island Bed is in the main channel just above the old bed, it is one of the best in the river, 500 yards in length, 150 yards in width, has a clean shelly bottom, and is easily worked.

Schnapper Point and *Rocky Point Beds*, unlike the two previous beds, have a broken and jagged bottom; being formed of slate rock set on edge, they can be worked only by the nippers or the double-shoe dredge. Spat caught in the crevices of these rocks cannot for the most part be disturbed even with this dredge, so that continual spatting goes on, and the bed is unattended by any risk from exhaustion.

Bold Shore Bed is 1,000 yards long but only 12 yards wide; the bottom is of shell and shingle; spat washed on to the shingle thrives there. The oysters, though not large, are of fair shape, and generally are in good condition. The shores also are, by natural formation, favourable to oyster growth.

Chinaman's Point Bed has two distinct formations: the upper end is of slate rock set on edge, while the lower end is of rock set horizontally, the foreshore being shingle; the upper end produces a green coloured cuppy shell, while the lower end shows a shell larger and flatter.

Dirty Lane Bed has a bottom of mud and shingle, and is somewhat soft; hence its name. The spat sets in bunches, the oysters occur in alternate stips separated by strips of mud.

Mogo Bend Bed is 900 yards long, and extends outwards from high-water mark for 40 yards, the bottom is shelly. Both the bed and shore are excellent for the culture of oysters which thrive luxuriously.

Big Island Bed is of large extent, 1 mile long by 100 yards wide. The bottom is broken and rocky, so much so that oysters can with difficulty be obtained even with the double-shoe dredge. They are safe from disturbance except by diving, as the depth of water precludes the profitable use of the tongs or nippers.

It will be scarcely fitting to close this chapter without a passing reference to the efforts put forth by Dr. Cox, the President of the Fisheries Commission, to create in the public mind an interest in oyster culture. The Colony is indebted to the Doctor for several valuable scientific papers on the subject, communicated either through the press or the agency of the Linnean Society, of which he has ever been a prominent member. Amongst the appendices is his paper on the Australian Oyster—it is full of information regarding the species and may be studied with profit by everyone professing an interest in the subject.

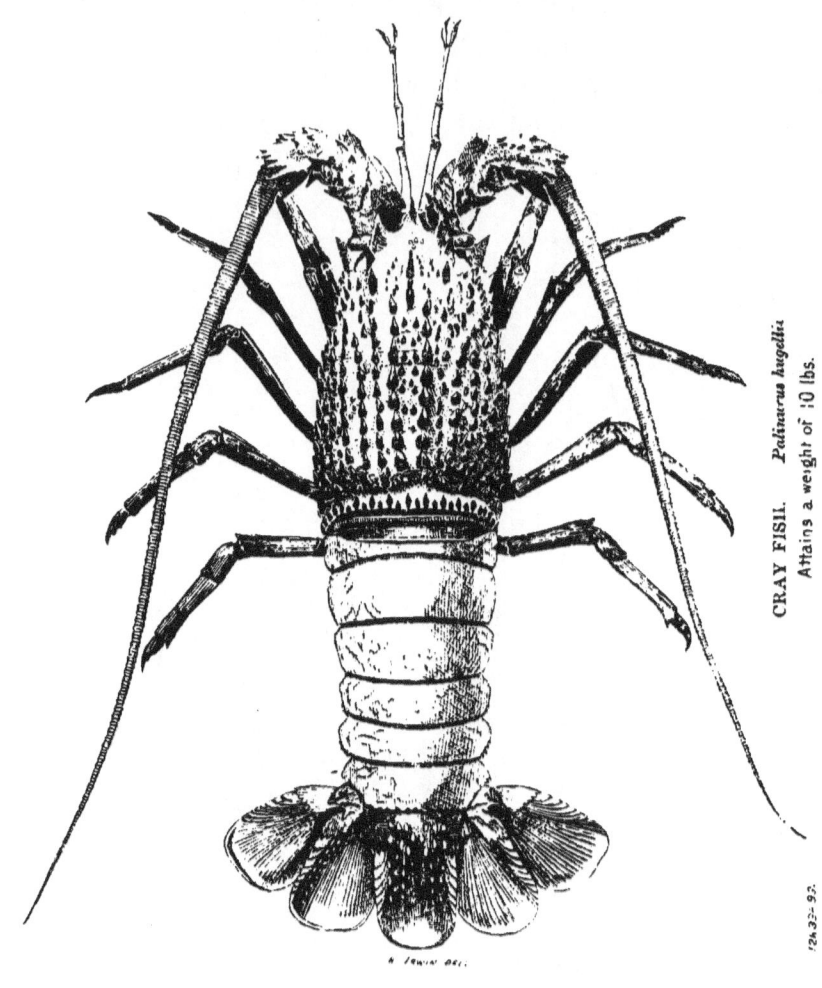

CRAY FISH. *Palinarus hugellii*
Attains a weight of 10 lbs.

CHAPTER VI.

CRUSTACEA.

The crustacea of New South Wales are numerous, only some of the species are in estimation as articles of food. The species principally sought after by fishermen is the large cray-fish (*Palinurus Hugellii*), the smaller cray-fish (*P. Lalandii*) known as the Tasmanian, the common prawn (*Penæus esculentus*), and the Murrumbidgee lobster (*Astacopsis spinifer*); the first named of these is about the finest of its kind. It attains a weight of 6 lb., and when in season is entirely filled with meat of the most excellent quality. It is found during the summer season abundantly along all parts of the coast, and is caught by means of circular nets from boats.

The mode of capture pursued in the early years of the Colony was by means of a bait rolled around a small stone attached to a strong cord, the bait was lowered into the water and the cray-fish taking it was hauled to the surface. This crude contrivance, which was very slow in its results, soon had to give place to the hoop-net, by means of which it was possible to load a boat with the fish in quite a short space of time. The change from the line to the net method of fishing was introduced by Thomas Mulhall, an old identity of Sydney Harbour. Mulhall now holds a position as Inspector of Fisheries.

In the early part of summer the ova are found within the abdomen of the female, when it is known to gourmets as the coral. The animal is then in the finest condition. About January the ova are shed, and are carried for a long time in a semi-hatched state on the underside of the tail or abdomen of the mother. Unfortunately the quality for food of the cray-fish does not seem to suffer much at this period, as is the case with crabs and other crustacea while undergoing the above process; the consequence is that the destruction of the young fish with the mother is going on during the entire season. The consumption in Sydney of this crustacean is very considerable, and the price generally high, but at times there is a glut in the market, and in consequence a serious fall in price. At the Broughton Islands, a few miles north of Port Stephens, the supply of this crustacean is unlimited. There are many parts of the coast too distant from Sydney for the supply of that market, where establishments for the "canning" of this valuable crustacean could be profitably undertaken. In this connection it may be noted that experimental attempts in the canning of this cray-fish have yielded most promising results.

Another species of cray-fish (*Palinurus Lalandii*) is often to be seen in the shop-windows of the Sydney fishmongers, but it chiefly comes from Tasmania. It is seldom found on the coast of New South Wales north of Twofold Bay. It is not nearly so large as the Sydney cray-fish, but is said to be equally valuable as food.

Of the true lobsters New South Wales can only boast of a very few, and these entirely confined to fresh water. Under the name "Marami" are included two or more species of *Astacopsis*, found in all the creeks and mud holes of the country. They are not much used as food, probably on account of their small size—seldom exceeding 4 or 5 inches in length, for they are as good to eat as any of the tribe.

One species, however, forms an exception to the others in point of size; it is the lobster of the Murrumbidgee and Murray system of Rivers—*Astacopsis spinifer*. This beautifully coloured lobster attains a considerable size, averaging a foot in length, and is esteemed a great delicacy. It is largely consumed by the residents on these rivers during the winter months—the season when they are in the best condition and most readily caught.

The prawn (*Penæus esculentus*) is abundant in most of our shallow bays and harbours, and is a most popular article of food amongst all classes. The consumption of this crustacean is so great that fears have been expressed that the supply might become exhausted, and it is undoubted that the size of some of those brought to market now is often much below the average of former years.

Another fine species of *Penæus* is found in the Murrumbidgee and the other western rivers. It is of fair size, and is said to be extremely good.

A species of *Alpheus* named the "Nipper" is abundant in Port Jackson, and is a good deal sought for, but not so much for food as for bait for black-bream fishing.

The following remarks respecting the breeding of prawns have been supplied by Mr. E. E. Bull, of Newcastle. Mr.

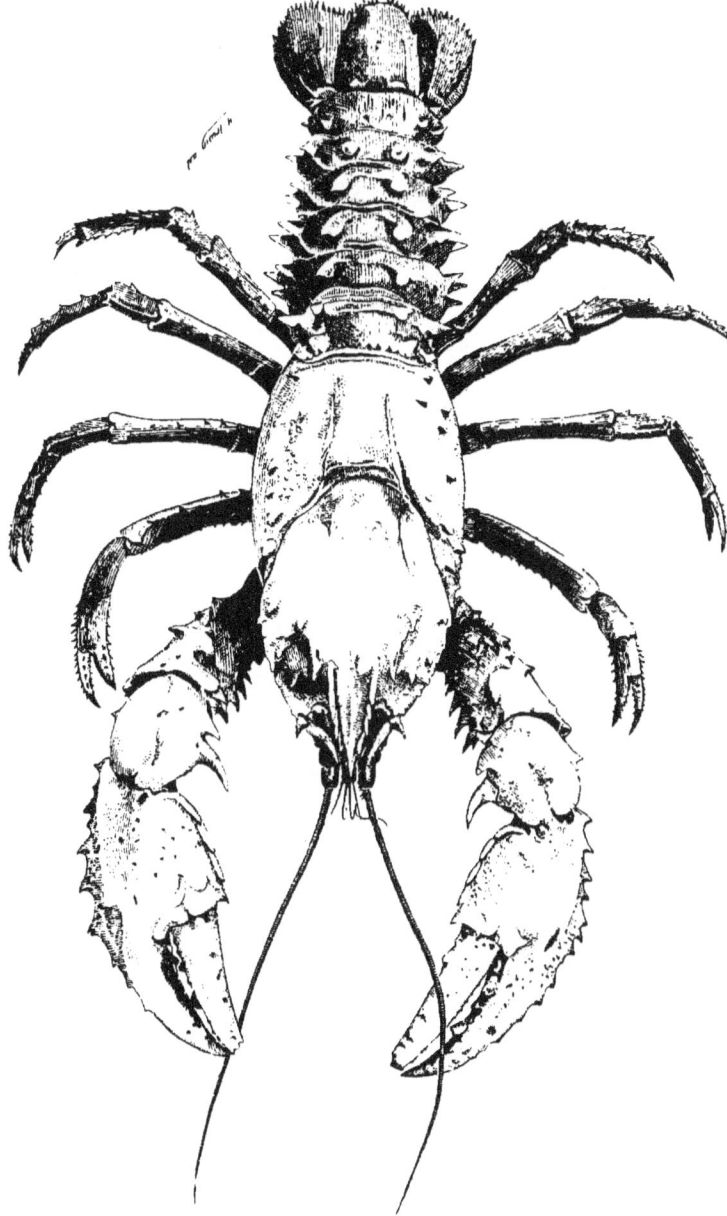

FRESHWATER LOBSTER. *Astacopsis spinifer.*
Attains a weight of 3 lbs.

Bull is a practical fisherman, and has always been an observer of nature, especially as regards fish and crustacea. He says that in the Hunter River there are two distinct species of prawn, commonly known among prawners as the yellow head or river prawn, and the white head or sea prawn. The former is very delicate as compared with the latter, and is rarely found nearer the mouth of the river than Hexham, excepting in flood times, as it appears to be partial to brackish rather than salt water, while the latter is rarely caught above Hexham, excepting in very dry seasons.

The yellow-head is not so good for market as the white, the latter is a larger species, its flesh is firmer, and it keeps longer.

Although they differ much in appearance, their mode of spawning and breeding is similar, and usually takes place between the months of February and May, but this is influenced considerably by the weather. When the spawn commences to mature, or appear on the legs, the prawn leaves its natural haunts or feeding-grounds, and travels up small creeks or drains into brackish water, swamps or marshes, where the spawning matures, after which the old prawns generally return to their regular feeding-grounds; but when they remain at the spawning place they attain an unusual size.

When the young prawns are about one-third grown they collect together in shoals and peregrinate towards the river in search of feeding-grounds, frequently accompanied by the old prawns that have remained behind.

I have frequently found them as far inland as the Hexham swamps, about 2 miles from either creek or river.

CHAPTER VII.

THE WHALE FISHERY.

The records of the whale fisheries are so incomplete that it has not been possible to find material for a succinct and connected account of their progress. A great deal of the matter which appears in the following pages has been gathered from a perusal of "Brett's Early New Zealand," and the writer gratefully acknowledges the assistance that work has afforded him.

The first notice of whaling at Sydney dates in August, 1790, when about the latter end of the month a spermaceti whale made its appearance in the harbour. A few days later another whale pursued a punt and overturned it, drowning a midshipman and two soldiers, and though its capture was attempted it escaped for the time, but eventually stranded in Manly Bay, and was killed by the natives.

Amongst the transport ships which arrived in Port Jackson during the year 1791 was the "Britannia," owned by the Messrs. Enderby, of London. On the voyage, after doubling the south-west coast of Van Diemen's Land, she sighted a large sperm whale off Maria Island, and more were met with within fifteen leagues of the latitude of Port Jackson. Within three leagues of the shore sperm whales were seen in numbers; the vessel passed through different shoals of them from noon of one day until after sunset; from the masthead shoals were visible all around the horizon. The crew were in the highest spirits at the sight, and the master, Thomas Melville, determined as soon as he had got rid of his living freight to make all possible despatch to this newly-found fishery.

On arrival, however, Captain Melville, had the misfortune to find that Governor Phillip wanted to despatch him with convicts to Norfolk Island. He thereupon related the account of the whales, thinking that it would release him from the projected visit, and advised that there was a prospect of establishing a fishery which might be of immense service to the Colony. Shortly afterwards the Governor sent for Melville and promised his assistance in despatching him to the fishery. The "Britannia" was accordingly the first ship ready for sea.

The secret of the whales, however, could not be kept from the other crews in port. It leaked out through the sailors, and all the vessels that could, viz., the "Mary Ann," the "Matilda," the "William and Anne," the "Salamander," and the "Britannia," embarked in the enterprise. The "Britannia" went to sea in company with the "William and Anne" on the eleventh day after arrival, and fell in with a great number of sperm whales; they were seen at sunrise all around the horizon. West, in his history of Tasmania, describes this as the discovery of the whale fishery in Australian waters. About the 10th November the "Britannia" and the "William and Anne" returned to port. The two vessels had killed, the day after their departure, seven sperm whales, but owing to bad weather succeeded only in securing two.

From the whale which fell to the share of the "Britannia," thirteen barrels of oil were obtained, mainly head matter (spermaceti). The master reported that he had seen, in ten days after his departure, fifteen thousand whales, the greater number of which were observed off Port Jackson. The report of the "Mary Ann" was not so encouraging. She had been as far south as 45° without seeing a whale, and in a gale of wind had shipped a sea that stove in two boats and washed down the brickwork-cased vessels intended for trying out the oil. The "Matilda" arrived in port a few days afterwards, having seen many whales, but was prevented by bad weather from killing any. The "William and Anne" returned a few days later, confirming the report of the great number of whales and the difficulty of getting at them. She had killed only one fish, and came in to repair and shorten her mainmast.

A difference of opinion prevailed amongst the masters of the ships respecting the possibility of establishing a whale fishery on this coast. In one particular, however, they were all agreed, which was that the coast abounded with fish; but the majority of the masters thought the currents and bad weather would prevent any of the ships from meeting with the success that was anticipated. However they determined upon another trial, and having made the necessary preparations again set out about the end of November. Early in December the "Matilda" and "Mary Ann" returned. Of whales, the "Matilda" saw none, but the "Mary Ann" was more fortunate. By going south she killed nine fish, securing five, which yielded thirty barrels of oil, when the weather became again bad. The vessels again sailed immediately after their arrival, and ran down south as far as 36° 30′, but returned on the 16th December, without killing a fish. The "Salamander" and "Britannia" arrived at the same time, reporting the same ill-fortune. Disheartened by these successive failures, the masters of some of the ships gave up all hopes of the establishment of a whale fishery in these seas; but the "Salamander" and "Britannia," on the 7th of January in the new year, started on a three months' cruise, with the intention at the expiration of that time, according to their success, either to return to Port Jackson or pursue their voyage north. From the absence, however, of further notice of the two vessels, it seems probable that their success was meagre, and that the expressed intention of going north was carried out.

In 1794 renewed efforts seem to have been put forth. Captain Melville, having again put in an appearance in Port Jackson, sailed on a trial voyage on the 2nd August of that year. He returned, however, without having seen a fish; subsequently he made repeated efforts with varying success.

On the 29th December, 1798, the "Indispensable" and "Britannia," which had been fishing on the coast for some time, appeared in port for repairs and to refresh their crews. They had cruised chiefly between the latitudes of 32° and 35°, not further from the coast than twenty to thirty leagues, and thought themselves tolerably sucessful for the time (only two months), the one having secured fifty-four and the other sixty tuns of spermaceti oil. Another vessel, the "Eliza" put into Botany Bay for wood and water, and, although much longer at sea than the other two, had secured only forty-five tuns of oil.

In March, 1799, the "Britannia" arrived again in Port Jackson with twenty-five tuns of sperm oil, the master reporting that had the weather been favourable he would have half filled his ship. On the 2nd June in the same year the "Diana" and "Eliza" arrived, each having twenty-five tuns. In October the "Eliza" was again in port wanting not more than thirty tuns to complete her cargo. In November the "Britannia" arrived with a complete cargo of oil. She appears to have been the first ship filled with sperm oil from Australian waters, as indeed eight years previously she had been the pioneer ship in the whaling industry.

The early failure, for such it certainly was, of the whale fishery on the Australian coast was attributable to two causes —the heavy weather which prevailed at the season of the year when the trials were made, and the ignorance of the masters of a coast hitherto so little frequented. However, upon the breaking out of the late war between Spain and England, the Spaniards of Peru and Chili fitted out privateers against the whalers on that coast. The greater part of these whalers, which had not expected, and consequently were not prepared against attacks of the kind, were compelled to abandon those seas and seek another scene for their adventures. It was, thereupon, resolved to make trial on the coast of New Holland. Four of the ships arrived in 1798, and their numbers so continued to increase that in the year 1800 there were quite twelve or fourteen, with cargoes averaging not less than from 150 to 160 tuns of oil, the current value of which amounted to between £180,000 and £190,000.

In later years the whale fisheries became of great importance. The year 1830 was an especially prosperous season. By the "Elizabeth," which arrived in Sydney on the 18th May from the whale fishery at the Bay of Islands, the news came that there were at the Bay ten vessels with full cargoes, besides two others spoken at sea. These were carrying a total quantity of 14,500 barrels, worth at a rough estimate about £120,000.

Sydney had now become a large whaling centre, with no less than twenty-two vessels sailing out of Port Jackson. In a paper published at the time it is recorded that, while three years previously New South Wales had but three vessels engaged in the whale fishery, altogether about 450 tons, at that present time she had 4,000 tons of shipping so employed.

Early in 1831 the "Elizabeth," belonging to Robert Campbell and Company, came into Sydney Harbour with 361 tuns sperm oil, the produce of an eighteen months' cruise. This was the most valuable cargo that had yet been brought into port—its estimated value being £21,600. In this year the whaling trade began to further expand, and black whale oil to swell the export.

Beyond the bare statements of the quantity of whale produce secured very little narrative concerning the incidents of the industry during succeeding years is available; the following table will show from a commercial point of view the value to New South Wales of the whale fisheries at that time and during the subsequent period it embraces.

Quantity of Whale oil, Whalebone, and Sealskins exported from New South Wales from the Year 1828 to 1840 inclusive, so far as can be ascertained from the incomplete returns obtainable :—

Year.	Sperm Oil.	Black oil.	Whalebone.		Sealskins.	Vessels.		Value.
	Tuns.	Tuns.	Tons	cwt.		Number	Tonnage	£
1828	311	28	0	17	8,723	......	......	27,011
1829	871 and 50 tuns head matter.	......	....		11,362	28	2,739	....
1830	983	98	9	16	9,720	32	3,687	50,471
1831	1,571	505	28	0	4,424	31	5,391	95,569
1832	2.491	695	43	0	1,415	20	3,497	147,409
1833	3,048½	418	27	0	1,890	27	6,922	146,855
1834	2,750¼	976	4	12	890	34	5,534	157,354
1835	2,904	1,159	108	0	667	22	5.162	180,439
1836	1,682	1,149	79	0	386	41	9,257	140,220
1837	2,559	1,565	77	8	107	......	......	183,122
1838	1,891	3,005	174	0	3 cases	......	......	197,644
1839	1,578	1,220	134	14	7	......	......	172,315

Number of Vessels engaged in Whale Fishing and Products obtained, 1840–1875.

Year.	No. of vessels engaged.	Products, quantity, and value.							Total Value.
		Sperm oil.		Black oil.		Whalebone.		Tortoiseshell and Sealskins.	
		Quantity.	Value.	Quantity.	Value.	Quantity.	Value.	Quantity.	Value.	
		tuns	£	tuns	£	cwt.	£	Sealskins. No.	£	£
1840	Not given.	1,304	102,313	1,589	26,309	2,160	6,403	324	537	135,562
1845	20	1,166	74,475	476	8,072	250	1,754	135	130	84,431
1850	37	958	45,087	382	4,015	......	......	......	......	49,102
								Tortoiseshell. lbs.	£	
1855	13	370	28,060	50½	2,000	......	......	800	720	30,780
1860	12	93½	6,539	210½	6,357	220	2,535	5,688	2,254	17,685
1865	3	130	7,110	130	7,085	0¾	10	3,893	2,639	16,844
1870	7	......	......	141	3,737	1	7	4,244	1,977	5,721
1875	2	13	1,040	80	3,450	40	808	... ..	......	5,298

Imports and Exports of Whale Oil and Whalebone,
1880, 1885, 1891 :—

Year	Vessels entered and cleared as whaling cruises.						Imports.						Exports.					
	Entered.			Cleared.			Sperm oil.		Black oil.		Whalebone.		Sperm oil.		Black oil.		Whalebone.	
	No. of Vessels.	Tons	Crews.	No. of Vessels.	Tons.	Crews.	Quantity.	Value.	Quantity.	Value.	Quantity.	Value.	Quantity.	Value.	Quantity.	Value.	Quantity.	Value.
							tuns	£	tuns	£	cwt.	£	tuns	£	tuns	£	cwt.	£
1880	...	...	...	...	...	...	1¾	123	142	4,384	...	...	...	...	8¾	286	52	206
1885	...	...	...	...	...	...	2¼	105	148	4,059	...	...	11½	550	26	911	26	315
1891	1*	531	15	1	531	44	5	151	219	5,536	35	1,999	7¾	220	10,½	274	33	1,825

* The result of this vessel's whaling cruise was 63 tuns of black oil, worth £1,525, and 17 cwt. whalebone, valued at £800. These figures are included in the total imports for that year.

From the year 1840 the whaling industry, so far as Sydney is concerned, began to decline. In searching for the cause of that decline the writer cannot perhaps do better than quote as an authority Captain J. B. Carpenter, the master of the "Costa Rica" packet. Captain Carpenter has been for many years engaged in the industry, his vessel having been for some time the only one belonging to the Colony employed in the whale fishery of the South Seas. To him and to Mr. H. Crummer, of the Royal Geographical Society of Australia, the writer is indebted for much of the information he has been able to collect respecting this industry. He says that for more than fifty years the American, French, and colonial whalers had been so constant and active in their pursuit of the whale in the Southern Ocean that the whales as a consequence became scarce and shy. In the year 1850 there were upwards of four hundred ships in the Southern Ocean alone, while in 1872 there were but seventy-two ships in the middle ground. This decline in the shipping so employed must have still further increased, for Captain Carpenter records that the whales having since that time been left unmolested have now multiplied to such an extent that those seas are fairly swarming with them. He relates that between September, 1887, and June, 1888, he met sperm whales on seventy-six different days, and that from

F

October, 1889, until December of the same year, he saw Right whales and Humpbacks on twenty-three different days. On the coast of New South Wales, from the latter end of April to the beginning of October, Right whales and Humpbacks are to be met with daily, and sperm whales all through the summer months.

That there is material for the development, in the immediate future, of an immense industry in connection with whaling in the Southern Seas, must be apparent to every one who has given ordinary thought to the matter. Captain Carpenter, who, at any rate as far as New South Wales is concerned, must be regarded as the pioneer in the attempt to revive this fishery, represents that the reports already taken home by traders have attracted the attention of those interested in the whaling industry in England, Europe, and America, resulting in the despatch of several vessels (four from Scotland and one from Norway, and perhaps others also not yet heard of) to the southern whaling grounds. These vessels left in September last and would reach the grounds about December, and when they return after successful voyages, as they almost certainly will, their reports will give a great impetus to the industry, and cause large numbers of vessels to be sent out to follow up the work that they have resumed in these Southern Seas.

"It is open to the business men of this port of Sydney not only to take part in this revival, and secure a share of the immense profits to be derived from the successful prosecution of whaling operations, but, also, it is possible to induce the greater number of the vessels forming the whaling fleets to make this port their depôt for disburdening themselves of the blubber and refitting for fresh cruises. If the Sydney people do not bestir themselves in this matter they will surely lose a magnificent opportunity of adding to the trade and importance of the Colony; and the advantages that should accrue to it from its specially favourable situation, in close proximity to the best whaling grounds in the world, will be secured by some other country— probably Valparaiso.

"Not only should steps be taken to send out whaling vessels hence, but works should be established for trying-out the blubber brought in by colonial or foreign ships. The industry could be initiated through the agency of a syndicate or company, which, by sending out two steam whalers, would thus create the nucleus of a local whaling fleet. The necessary vessels could be purchased in Scotland at present for less than a third of their real value—as a matter of fact, suitable vessels, which could not be built for £30,000, have recently been offered for sale for £6,000—but if matters are delayed until the return of the whalers recently sent out from the other side of the world, it will be next to impossible to obtain anything in the shape of a suitable steamer except at very heavy cost. A small capital would suffice to purchase and fit out the vessels and keep things going for the first voyage, and after that all would be perfectly plain sailing.

"The advantage of making Sydney a depôt for carrying on the whaling industry lies in the fact that it is handy to both the summer and winter whaling grounds, and the vessels fitting out hence may practically avoid all idle time. Black whales are plentiful all along our coast in the winter from 1st April to 1st October, while in the summer the steam whalers could go down to as far as 62° for the right whales, which abound in those waters. With steam whalers the whales could be followed up amongst the ice without great risk, such as precluded the old type of sailing ship from going too far south, while profit is also to be derived from hunting the seals and sea elephants that are to be easily got at on the breaking up of the ice in these regions. Thousands of these animals were seen by Ross in his voyages near Victoria Land, due south of Sydney. Steam whalers could leave here about October, and follow up right whaling in the southern latitudes up to February, and return to Sydney in plenty of time to unload and refit for the winter whaling along our coasts, at the Kermadec Islands or in the neighbourhood of the Bampton Shoals.

"As to the profits to be made out of whaling, the prospects seem brighter than ever they were. Whales are, according to the reports to hand recently, plentiful enough to make good voyages almost a certainty; and if whaling paid when bone was worth only £150 per ton, it ought to produce fortunes at present when its market price is £3,000 per ton. After careful calculation, and fully allowing for all contingencies, Captain Carpenter finds that a capital of £20,000 would suffice to equip two steam whalers, and that the first voyage to the south ought to produce a net profit of nearly £20,000. He claims that no enterprise at the present moment can show anything like the same prospects of profit as that he is so anxious to see entered upon.

"The cost of establishing oil-boiling works in Sydney would be small, while the advantages to be gained, both in the matter of affording employment and adding to the trade of the port, would be considerable. The practice of whalers is to strip the blubber from the whales and stow it in tanks fitted into the ships, bringing it to their depôts in that state to be tried out. If the industry is revived in these Southern Seas, Sydney would have a splendid opportunity of centering the whole of this trying-out work on the spot, because, if the ships could come here within a few days' steam from the fishing grounds and get their blubber tried out, they would certainly do so in preference to carrying it all the way to Dundee or other equally distant ports at which trying-out is now carried on.

"Much more could be said upon this subject, but sufficient has been stated to show that the matter is worthy of careful consideration, and it is hoped that some enterprising colonist will take the matter up and give it a practical turn."

The ranges of the different species of whales and the places they frequent, together with the seasons in which they are to be found, are shown in the accompanying chart* which Captain Carpenter has been good enough to supply. It will be seen from it that the habitat of the Right whale, which is of the same species as the Arctic or Greenland whale, is from 34° south latitude to within the Antarctic circle. The sperm whale in the southern hemisphere is found between the equator and south as far as the 63rd parallel of latitude. The Rarqual or Sulphur-bottom whale and fin-back extend from the equator to the south polar regions. The Humpback is not found at all between the 15th degree of south latitude and the equator, its range being from that parallel to the Antarctic circle. The sperm whales in the tropical latitudes are mostly small, their yield being from 30 to 70 barrels of oil; but from 30° south to the Antarctic ocean they grow to an enormous size, yielding as much as 165 barrels each. The Right whale that visits the New South

---

See Appendices.

Wales coast is generally of the size to yield from 10 to 12 tuns of oil and about half a ton of balleen, but further south the whales are very large, often yielding as much as 18 tuns of oil, and balleen fully fifteen feet long, and weighing about 15 cwt. or 16 cwt.

The residents at Norfolk Island, though not possessing any ships, manage to kill a few whales during the year by means of boats, and export thence to Sydney about 40 tuns of black oil and variable quantities of whalebone. Quite recent accounts tell us that the islanders have suffered a severe loss, two of their boats having been smashed into matchwood and four others badly stove. The season now closing has not therefore been as prosperous as it otherwise would have been. Whales have been more than usually plentiful, but a number which were struck were lost owing to the absence of boats, and these numerous misses have told seriously against the exceptionally good take which was anticipated.

The residents at Twofold Bay, on the south-eastern coast of the Colony, pursue a similar method, and their yearly capture forms a tangible item in the trade of the locality.

About the year 1846 this bay was the anchorage for numerous whaling vessels which put in there to refit. On the south side was the large whaling establishment of Mr. Benjamin Boyd, whence nine sperm whalers used to sail.

When it is considered that Great Britain with all her colonies had at that time only fifty-nine vessels engaged in the trade, which in the Pacific Ocean alone employed nearly 700 American whalers, a very correct estimate of the comparative value of the depôts at Twofold Bay can be easily formed. The produce of the whaling operations in 1846 was estimated at—

500 tuns sperm oil, value … …	£36,100
200 ,, black oil ,, … …	4,000
10 tons whalebone ,, … …	1,500
	£41,600

A very interesting feature which should be noted in connection with the prosecution of this industry was the advance in civilization made by the aborigines of the district. It is on record that they proved themselves an active, intelligent race, and in their useful labour in boating and the various arduous employments on board the whalers they contradicted the hasty conclusions which so many superficial writers had drawn in reference to the degrading tendency of the faculties of the natives of New South Wales.

Mr. Benjamin Boyd, who originated the whaling industry at Twofold Bay, was the descendant of an ancient Scottish family. He arrived in Sydney in the year 1841 commissioned to organise branches of business for the Royal Banking Company of Australia. In making a settlement at Twofold Bay he had some of these objects in view. In the first place he built a large store for the purpose of supplying his extensive sheep stations in the Monaro district; he also erected a boiling-down plant, and in addition to these and other matters as well, he entered largely into whaling, and fixed the Bay as the rendezvous for his ships. On the south head he constructed a light-house for the purpose of directing his vessels coming to the wharf; but this scheme proved abortive as the New South Wales Government refused to permit the exhibition of a light unless a guarantee were given for its constant maintenance. Mr. Boyd seems to have been possessed of unusual enterprise and pluck, but somehow his efforts did not secure that pecuniary success which they deserved, and so at last the Company who had all along provided the capital for the immense business which was being carried on began to manifest uneasiness in regard to it, and ultimately grew so dissatisfied that a change in the management was demanded. After prolonged negotiations a compromise was effected—Boyd agreed to retire and to relinquish all claims upon the Company in consideration of receiving three of the whale ships, two sections of land at Twofold Bay and his yacht the "Wanderer," a vessel of some 80 tons burthen, in which he had sailed hither from England. Boyd's ultimate fate was sad. He embarked with a gold digging party, mostly consisting of Australian Aborigines on board the "Wanderer," and sailed for California in 1850, the time of the gold excitement there. His venture was unsuccessful, and on his way back to Sydney he touched at Guadalcanar, one of the islands in the Solomon Group; there he went on shore with a black boy to have some shooting, and it is supposed he was murdered by the natives as he was never seen again.

THE WHALE.

A brief account of the whale may be of interest. The sperm whale contains in its head, in the fluid state, the spermaceti of commerce. This whale sometimes reaches the length of seventy or eighty feet, the head forming about one-half of the entire animal. The head is called by the whalers the case, and is divided into compartments communicating with each other. The "head matter" is nearly pure sperm, fluid in consistency as blood, and is laden out of the head of the fish with buckets fashioned for the purpose. A large whale will carry in its case ten or fifteen barrels—a barrel contains about thirty gallons. Between the case and upper jaw lies a large mass of blubber, which yields nearly double the quantity obtained from the "case." When cold the spermaceti hardens and assumes a somewhat snowy flakey appearance. A large sperm whale has been known to yield as much as a hundred and thirty barrels, which would have realised in some seasons as much as £1,250. When Europeans first came to the Western Pacific seas the sperm whale was found in large numbers all round the coasts, but experience has made the survivors wary, and they are now as a rule to be found only in deep water. They swim under the surface of the water at the rate of from three to seven miles an hour; but on being alarmed will dive, and afterwards rise slowly in a perpendicular position, with their blunt heads more or less above the surface, in apparently a listening attitude, remaining in that position for fully half an hour, scarcely moving. An almost electrical communication is at times perceptible amongst them. A school of upwards of one hundred have been seen spread over the ocean as far as the eye from the mast-head could reach, when on one of the number being lanced, an instantaneous disappearance of the whole school took place, all diving with great celerity and in concert.

The Right or black whale of the Southern Seas is somewhat inferior in size to its congener the Greenland whale. In regard to their economy they are said to be almost alike. It is from this animal that the whalebone of commerce is obtained. Unlike the sperm whale it has no teeth, but in the upper jaw of its enormous head, which is some 15 to 20 feet long, 10 to 12 feet high, and 6 to 8 feet broad, presenting when the mouth is open a cavity as large as a room, are fixed plates of baleen, about 300 in each row, which, spreading outwards, enclose at their lower end the large, soft, immovable tongue, giving an ideal resemblance to the canvas falling from the tent-pole over a monster feather-bed. The baleen itself originates from a thin, fleshy substance resting on the gum, which affords a continuous supply of the material requisite for its wonderful after-growth. The whalebone reaches in the larger animals from 9 to 12 feet in length ; it is externally of a gray or greenish colour, while the fine fibrous filaments proceeding from its inner edge are black. These latter form a thick internal covering, which, acting as a screening apparatus, permits no particle within it to escape, but imprisons and sifts the small but extremely abundant creatures, composed of shrimps, crabs, sea-snails, and other minute marine objects, more commonly known by the term whale-brit, which form the food of this monster of the deep.

The price of oil from the sperm whale realised sometimes three times as much as that from the Right or black whale. The ships first employed in the South Sea fishery varied in tonnage, from one hundred to five hundred tons, and were calculated to carry from eight hundred to five thousand barrels of oil. They were fitted with try works or fireplaces containing two or three iron pots, each pot holding from one hundred and fifty to two hundred gallons. The fireplace was made of bricks, so laid as to preserve the deck from damage. The water was confined in a square formed of planking. When the cargo was completed, or the ship full, the fireplaces were taken down and the pots stowed away. In these pots the blubber was treated *i.e.* boiled or fried— the mincing of the blubber being an important factor in the easy extraction of the oil. The fires were fed principally from whale scraps, the animal thus providing fuel to extract his own grease. After the blubber had been sufficiently tried, the oil was baled out and placed in coolers, generally made of copper, to cool and settle, when it was put into casks holding about thirty gallons, called barrels, or into larger vessels holding about two hundred and eighty gallons, called tuns. A whaler of 350 tons would make use of four boats and carry two spare ones.

CHAPTER VIII.
THE PEARL-SHELL FISHERIES.

Though the region of the pearl-shell fisheries, confined as it principally is to the tropical coast-line of Australia, is altogether remote from the territorial limits of this Colony, a desire has been expressed that a passing notice of them should appear in this pamphlet, inasmuch as the industry is to a large extent owned and worked by persons resident here with a fleet of one hundred and thirty boats.

Mr. Saville Kent, at the time Commissioner of Fisheries for Queensland, in his official report for 1888, thus describes these boats, and furnishes the further particulars concerning the trade which are subjoined :—

"The vessels employed in the Queensland pearl-shell fishery consist chiefly of strong lugger-rigged craft, averaging ten tons burden, supplemented in some instances by cutters of larger size, which serve as purveyors to the luggers, and to bring the shell collected into port. The crews manning these luggers comprise the diver, who takes command and acts as sailing master; one tender, who holds the life lines and attends to all signals from the diver at his work; and four working hands, who in pairs take alternate shifts at the manual pumping apparatus for supplying air to the diver. With but few exceptions the entire crews consist of coloured men of various nationalities; mainland aboriginals, South Sea Islanders, and natives from the Torres Straits Islands furnish the greater number, while some of the best divers are represented by Chinese, Japanese, and Malays. The few European divers are mostly the proprietors of their own boats. The shelling luggers are usually provisioned for one month, but may stay out longer, having the requisite stores brought to them by the cutters. The primary cost of a fully equipped pearl-shelling lugger, of (say) 10 tons, averages £650, out of which £150 may be set off as the price of the diving apparatus and pumping gear. The wages earned by the crews are as follows :—The diver, from £2 to as much as £4 10s. per 100 pairs of shells raised, £3 being a common average. The tender receives £3, and the four pumping hands £2 10s. each per month. Rations for the entire crew average about £9 monthly. The cost of maintenance, including wages and rations, but not the diver's earnings, which necessarily vary, may therefore be set down at an average of £22 for the month.

"Mr. Kent says a fairly remunerative quantity of shell for a boat to bring in as the result of one month's work is from 600 to 700 pairs, and which consisting of, or reckoned as, 3-lb. shell, would represent but little short of a ton in weight. In fine weather, and under exceptionally favourable conditions, as much as from 1,200 to 1,800 pairs may be obtained, and it is the custom among certain of the station owners and boat proprietors to give the divers and crews a bonus for all shell collected numbering over 1,000 pairs. The agreement with the divers in reckoning up the number of shell brought in is usually to count it as 2-lb. or 3-lb. shell, such terms signifying that all the pairs of shells as they are naturally attached must weigh not less than 2 lb. or 3 lb. each. Any pairs short of this weight have other shells added, until the standard weight is arrived at. In the case of a very small shell, it may take three pairs or six shells to make up the 3 lb., or even seven pairs to complete 6 lb., or a standard two pairs, which are usually weighed in at once. £200 per annum, in addition to his rations, represents a fair average income for a diver to earn.

"The average depth of water from which the greater quantity of the mother-of-pearl shell is at present collected is seven or eight fathoms. In former years it was abundant, and is even now occasionally obtained in water of such little depth that it can be gathered with the hand at low spring tides. Twenty fathoms of water represent about the greatest depth from which the shell is profitably fished, though but few divers can stand the strain of prolonged work at this depth. Some of the largest shell now placed on the market is collected at the above depth from off the New Guinea coast.

"The head-quarters of the Pearl-shell Fisheries of Queensland are at Thursday Island, Torres Straits, $10\frac{1}{2}$ degrees S. lat., 140 degrees E. long., and thirty miles north-west of Cape York, the northernmost point of the Australian continent. All the licenses for vessels, boats, and men employed in this fishery are taken out at Port Kennedy in Thursday Island; and from this centre shelling expeditions are made along the mainland coast-line to the northern limits of the Great Barrier Coral Reef, and throughout Torres Straits northwards to the vicinity of New Guinea.

THE PEARL-SHELL FISHERIES.

"The pearls obtained from the Queensland pearl-shell fisheries do not, under existing conditions, constitute a recognised source of income to the boat and station owners. The fishery is conducted exclusively for the sake of the shell, and while the pearls obtained belong rightfully to the proprietors of the boats, they are so extensively appropriated by the divers and boats' crews as to have become practically their perquisite. The pearls of Torres Straits are generally represented as being less numerous and inferior in quality in comparison with those of West Australia. At the same time pearls of very considerable value are of by no means rare occurrence in Queensland waters, and the boat and station owners have beyond question a just cause of complaint at being so systematically deprived of their rightful property. It is advocated by many of the boat proprietors that stringent regulations should be enacted, restricting the traffic in pearls to licensed agents only.

"The average price realised for pearl-shell is £125 per ton gross, or £100 net, while the common all-round price at which the shell is bought in by leading mercantile firms stationed at Thursday Island is £90 per ton. In former years the price for shell of good quality ranged as high as £200 per ton; the shell itself was more readily accessible and obtained at less cost, and the profits in the trade were consequently much more considerable. Twenty years ago, immediately previous to the discovery of the West Australian shelling grounds, prices as high as £16 and £20 per cwt., or from £320 to £400 per ton, were realised for the best Manilla shell. At the present time the best shell in the market is obtained from Torres Straits."

The following are the names and owners of vessels registered at the Port of Sydney, New South Wales, engaged in the Pearl-shell Fishing Trade:—

Names of Vessels.	Tonnage.	Registered Owners.
Christina Gollau	37	William Villiers Brown.
Hiroshima	11	
Nana	11	
Wild Colonial	13	
Arethusa	9	Burns, Philp, & Co. (Limited).
Constitution	8	
Clara Merriman	15	
May	7	
Pioneer	11	
Princess	9	
Sana	8	

Names of Vessels.	Tonnage.	Registered Owners.
Ceres	10	James Burns.
Billy J. C.	9	} Frederick John Gibbins.
Carrie	16	
Chris	8	
F.L.J.	9	
G.P.	8	
Hercules	8	
Hero's Luck	9	
Rover	12	
Syren	10	
Vision	13	
Endeavour	9	} Thomas Gervin Kelly.
Enterprise	10	
Johnny	10	
Kirkham	12	
Nixie	12	
Narellan	12	
North Star	12	
Pearl Queen	14	
Pearl King	13	
Vailele	11	
Celia	8	
Shamrock	9	} John Alfred Reddell.
Britannia	9	
Ethel	180	
Bingie	9	} William Robison.
Mars	8	
Maggie	9	
Narelle	9	
Orion	8	
Pearl	65	
Polly	9	
Sirius	7	
Mist	92	
Dauntless	24	} Joseph Tucker.
Daisy	10	
Kate	16	
Lilly	10	
Monarch	9	
Revenge	17	
Young Australia	6	
Annie	6	} John De V. Lamb, John Broomfield, joint owners.
Alice	7	
Barb	7	
Beatrice	11	
Cambria	11	
Gertrude	12	
Henrietta	11	
Ida	12	
Johnny & Annie	9	
Kafoa	11	

THE PEARL-SHELL FISHERIES.

Names of Vessels.	Tonnage.	Registered Owners.
Magic	7	John De V. Lamb, John Broomfield, joint owners.
Martha	8	
Marjorie	10	
Rosa	8	
Two Brothers	16	
Wai Weer	29	
Xarifa	11	
Eleanor	13	
Dayspring	159	Frederick John Gibbins, Francis Buckle, John Paul, joint owners.
Kestrel	8	Thomas Littlejohn, Reginald Edmund Finlay, joint owners.
Pearl Hunter	8	Henry Blakesley, Robert Hunter, joint owners.
Missie	24	William Wood, Thomas Glover, joint owners.
Bertha	11	Albert Kollisch, John Molloy, joint owners.
Dart	15	Neil Christian Anderson, managing owner.
Topsy	12	John Walker, managing owner.
Sagitta	84	James Clark, ,,
Mamoose	7	Charles M'Alister, ,,
Look Out	108	George Cockburn, ,,
Eleanor	12	James Tait, ,,
Freya	13	Andrew Anderson.
Jenny	12	Neil Christian Anderson.
Little Nell	8	John Bell.
Minerva	12	Herbert Bowden.
Sapphire	13	Walter S. Boore.
Storm King	9	Carey Buswell.
Centennial	9	Neil Christian Christiansen.
Ena	9	James Clark.
Juno	7	Rebecca Cussen.
Marama	8	
Mary Cussen	11	
Rosina	10	Stephen Clark.
Carrie	6	David Scott Elliott.
Ellen	13	Mary Ann Icca.
Congho	14	Thomas Lewthwaite Grainger.
Francisco	14	
Flora	15	
Mabel	14	
Rotumah	14	
Wybenia	13	
Savo	19	Samuel Keating.

Names of Vessels.	Tonnage.	Registered Owners.
Bantam	10	⎫
Curlew	10	⎪
Gamecock	8	⎪
Gannet	10	⎬ Thomas Littlejohn.
Goshawk	10	⎪
Jessamine	8	⎪
Petrel	8	⎭
Chloe	10	Edward Larsen.
Whaup	35	Emanuel Franz Lichtner.
Clio	7	⎫ James Merriman.
Thistle	6	⎭
Cupid	12	Christopher Macrae.
Elsea	35	Thomas Mullan.
Jane	11	John Molloy.
Lizzie	7	John Moreman.
Rebecca	6	Walter Joseph Munro.
Sylph	12	Thomas M'Nulty.
William	6	Robert Moodie.
Activity	62	Pearling Trading Co. (Ltd.)
Sedney	14	Hans Christian Rasmussen.
Endymion	10	⎫ George Smith.
Vera	10	⎭
Harriet	50	Emile Sirie.
Little Frank	6	George Alexander Smythe.
Agnes	7	Charles Tuckfield.
Coral Sea	16	Colin Thomson.
Wikingen	7	⎫ Charles Thorngren.
Mayri	7	⎭
Total	2,172	

CHAPTER IX.
ABORIGINAL FISHERIES.
Contributed by E. G. W. Palmer.

Fish, in almost all its edible forms, including molluscs and crustacea, must always have formed a very important item in the bill of fare of the Australian Aborigines, and have been the great standby of many of the principal tribes. This is clearly evidenced by the "Kitchen Middens" along the shores of many of our rivers and estuaries, and the rock shelters or caves around Port Jackson present, on even a casual investigation, abundant proof that fish and oysters, with other marine products, entered largely into the daily cuisine of the tribes who held sway here before the white men took their place. Considerable ingenuity was exercised by them in obtaining supplies, and many devices were used according to the class of fish to be taken and the character of the waters they frequented. Probably the greatest quantity was obtained by the use of the muttock or three or four pointed fish-spear. Where the water was shallow they would wade about on the mud flats spearing the mullet, whiting, bream, and flatheads as they came within range, or, in deeper waters they would float in their bark canoes striking the larger fish with a dexterity born of long practice and the promptings of a healthy appetite. Spearing fish by torchlight was a device often practised by them, and in Port Stephens, when the tribes were numerous, I have seen a number of canoes in which the gins held the flaming firesticks while their husbands darted their muttocks at the fish attracted by the light. Some of the tribes were good net-makers, and they also fabricated hooks of sharp splinters bones and shells which served their purpose fairly well, but have now been discarded for hooks of European manufacture. Nettle-bark, Kurrajong, and various other fibrous plants were used to make their fishing-lines and the twine or cordage of their nets. On the Clarence, and probably elsewhere, they pounded up certain plants and barks which they cast into the waterholes and creeks, making the water so obnoxious to the fish that they speedily came to the surface and were made an easy prey. Eels would glide from the water and hide among the grass and sedge and the fish would make every effort to get beyond the influence of the noxious drug. Of course the destruction of small fry was very great where this plan was adopted. Traps of various kinds were fabricated by some tribes. Some of these are of basket-work and resemble eel traps; others were more complicated and were placed in running streams. In tidal waters enclosures were made with stakes and interwoven sticks and brushwood having openings which were closed at high water, and similar contrivances were often to be seen at the embouchures of small creeks and back waters in which, at times, considerable quantities of shoal fish were taken. Almost everything "was fish that came to their nets," but I am not aware whether, like the Chinese, they considered stingrays' flappers and dried sharks' fins a special delicacy. The liver of the large porcupine fish certainly was deemed a tit bit. I believe it is generally considered to be a poisonous fish as it belongs to a genera that contains many dangerous species.

A gentleman resident on the Murrumbidgee described in graphic terms an afternoon spent with several blacks on a fishing excursion when a large take of Murray cod was obtained by the men diving into deep water and spearing the cod with short spears while below the surface. The cod were apparently very numerous and of great size and were probably in a more quiescent state than usual. He stated that it was by no means an uncommon mode of obtaining fish by the Waradgeric blacks.

The most remarkable method of catching river-fish is that adopted by the tribes on the Barwon or Darling River, at Brewarrina, and it is probably unique so far as the Australian Aborigines are concerned.

At Brewarrina, which is a small township about 70 miles above Bourke on the Darling River, and some 530 miles from Sydney, there is a structure of Aboriginal workmanship of undated antiquity, and possibly the only work of a permanent character known to have had its origin among this race. At this part of the river its course is obstructed by a granitic dyke which forms a natural dam when the waters of the river fall below a certain level. Above this dyke the depth of water is considerable for a long stretch of the river, and the upper waters and branches of the river are well stocked with cod, perch, and other fish. For some distance down the river its bed is strewn with great boulders, and the stream restrained by the dyke is under ordinary circumstances a shallow rapid,

The Brewarrina Fishery.

though, when the Darling is in flood, there is depth sufficient for the river steamers to pass to and fro. The fish in their migrations up and down the river must negotiate the rapids and some astute Aboriginal of bygone times having probably found a dinner in the shape of a weighty cod (they grow to 60 or 100 lb. weight) temporarily resting in a little pool among the boulders, gradually evolved the idea that if better pools were made more cod would be obtainable. The "Fisheries," as they now exist, are of considerable extent, and the ownership of different sections is clearly defined by tribal understanding. The rocky bottom of the rapid has been cleared of boulders which have been built up into roughly-constructed walls, forming pools or yards of varying dimensions and shapes, some being long and narrow, others nearly square, and others again curved or of irregular shape. Whatever the shape, the design is the same in each case, namely, to hamper the movements of the fish and secure as many as possible for use as food.

The blacks, who now enjoy the benefits of the "Fisheries," have no very reliable account to give of its construction. When asked, "Who been first time make it?" some of the old men replied: "Baal! I know; you see that all a same long time. Old fellow black been make him murry long time ago." They stated that several different tribes had the right of fishing, but they could only take fish from their own yards. So long as there is a flow of water in the river, fish in varying quantities may be obtained; but it is immediately on the fall of the river, after a heavy flood, that the great harvest is obtained. When the water is high the fish are dived for. When the river is about its normal height, the blacks wade in and spear or net the fish. There are generally a few old blacks camped on either side of the river in small camps of bark-gunyahs or break-winds of bushes, and they appear to watch their tribal interests, and repair the walls when requisite. If fish are plentiful the other members of the tribe gather at the "Fisheries"; if scarce, they go up or down the river, or hunt in the plains at a distance.

One feature of the "Fisheries" is the immense number of aquatic birds of a predatory character which frequent it. Cormorants, divers, grebes, &c., are always in great force, besides spoonbills, cranes, crows, and others which appear to find a good feeding-ground, so that the destruction of young

G

fish must be very great. One of the blacks was asked why they did not shoot the divers and stop them eating the fish, to which he replied with true aboriginal humour, "Well, you see that only 'nother fellow blackfellow and that must eat," but at a later visit I saw a diver being roasted at one of the camp fires.

The "Fisheries" must always be a matter of interest to the student of Australian ethnology, enshrouded as its first construction is in mystery, and from the fact that, although the Brewarrina fishery has proved such a lasting and continuous success, it does not appear that any similar construction has ever been attempted elsewhere.

CANOES AND FISHING.

From "Notes on the Aborigines of Australia."

By John F. Mann.

The management of a bark-canoe is perhaps as remarkable a feat as that of tree-climbing.

In constructing a canoe a suitable tree is selected, generally a stringy-bark. Two horizontal rings are cut round the tree through the bark, at a distance apart of 8, 10, or 12 feet, and a perpendicular cut down one side enables the whole sheet to be carefully removed. The rough exterior is pared off, leaving the thin, hard inside shell. It is then placed over a fire; this enables the ends to be gathered up and folded. Sharp sticks like skewers are passed through these folds, and secured by cords or bands of bark. The opening of the canoe is preserved by stretchers or sticks placed across.

Whilst stripping the bark from the tree, the black makes use of a ladder, formed by cutting notches in a strong forked sapling, which is leant against the tree.

These canoes support a very considerable load. With a blackfellow alone they draw but a few inches of water. Being perfectly round at bottom, having no keel, they overturn with the slightest movement; yet in these frail canoes I have known blacks to make wonderful journeys. A settler on the Clyde, many years ago, engaged a black and his canoe to remove all his effects from one side of the river to the other. I saw him with a heavy bullock plough in his canoe. After removing farm implements and furniture, he removed several tons of potatoes, his canoe being but an inch or two above the water on each trip. One old man, white with age when I knew him, seemed to have passed his life in one. He would traverse Lake Macquarie and go out into the open sea; from this lake he would carry his canoe across the neck of land separating it from Tuggerah Beach Lake, thence to Brisbane Water, and across Broken Bay to Pittwater, and made periodical visits up the Hawkesbury River. He was never without fish in his canoe, which was often so laden as to be only a few inches above the water. This old man, "Jew-fish" by name, eventually became so cramped that when on shore he could retain no other position than that which sitting in a canoe compelled him to adopt. I have also known the blacks at Bateman's Bay to go out as far as the Tollgate Islands. They are often pursued by sharks, when they paddle away for the nearest shore, throwing over as they go along any fish they may happen to have.

The blackfellow, whilst fishing from his canoe, which he does by means of a spear, sits on his haunches, his right leg doubled under him, his left knee drawn up to his shoulder. In his right hand he carries his "wammerah" or throwing-stick, formed to serve as a paddle; in his left a small piece of flat wood, also as a paddle, whilst his fishing-spear lies across in front of him, ready for use. On spearing a fish he paddles up to his spear, and instead of pulling it out at once gives it another thrust in, so as to ensure its capture. As refraction causes a difference between the true and apparent position of the fish, great practice is necessary. They seldom miss their object.

Women also fish from canoes, but with a hook and line; they never use a spear. They fix the canoe in position along the edge of a bank by driving the long pointed stick, which they invariably carry, into the sand or mud. They then pass one of their arms round the pole, or tie the canoe to it, so as to steady it. By means of a flat stone and clay for a hearth, they can light a fire and cook fish. They are often accompanied by one or more children, who have to remain very quiet.

A fishing-spear consists of a grass-tree shaft with four long prongs of hardwood inserted at one end of it. Sometimes the stem of the gigantic lily is used, but this is not so strong or so durable as the grass-tree. The test as to the fitness of the grass-tree for this purpose is the manner in which it breaks off from the stem of the tree. It is never cut with a tomahawk, and must not be either too green or too dry.

In constructing a spear, two splits are made at one end of the stick, at right angles, and the pith extracted to the depth of 3 or 4 inches. This end is then bound round with ribbon-like strips of bark, obtained from a small shrub or from the kurryjong tree. The aperture is then filled with grass-tree gum, a resin having much the appearance of gamboge in its pure state, but as generally used it is not unlike pitch, in consequence of the effects of exposure to the smoke of bush fires. Into this, whilst in a soft state, the four prongs, slightly tapered at the end, are pressed. This has the effect of forcing much of the gum through the splits and through the band of bark, when by holding it near the fire, the gum is neatly spread over the joints. These prongs, which are from 15 to 18 inches long, are scraped to a fine point, and barbed by means of a small splinter of bone fastened to the end. The four points of this spear form a square about 1 inch or more apart, and are kept in position by small wedges of wood passed between the prongs and fastened by bands of ribbon bark. The pith from the other end of the spear is extracted to the depth of about an inch, the end is bound with twine, and the whole stopped with the fine scrapings of hardwood, which serves as a pad for the hook of the "wammerah," or throwing-stick, to press against. Other grass-tree spears are made in a similar manner, but with only one prong. In those parts where the grass-tree does not exist, the spear is made of one long straight piece of wood, which is cut from the side of a standing tree.

The "wammerah," a stick by means of which the spear is thrown, is about 3 feet long, in shape something like a long-handled spoon; the spoon, a rather flat part, being used as a paddle when fishing from a canoe; at the opposite end a short piece of stick is fastened so as to form a hook. In throwing a spear, the broad end of the wammerah is held across the palm of the hand, with the point of the hook pressing against the pad in the end of the spear, the spear at the same time being held firmly between the forefinger and thumb. By the use of the stick, great force and impetus is given to it, and makes it a much more formidable weapon than those spears which are made from one piece of wood and are thrown by the hand as darts. Occasionally these spears have sharp splinters of quartz or of glass fastened along one side. Solid spears are frequently made with one or more barbs. In those parts of the country where the wammerah is not required as a paddle, they are formed from one stick, the hook being the natural fork of the branch.

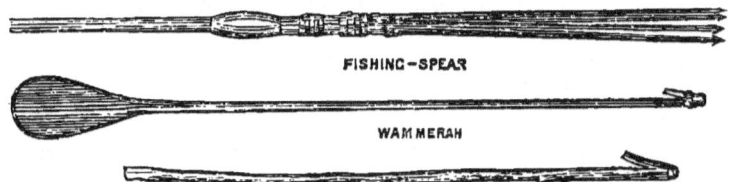

FISHING-SPEAR

WAMMERAH

APPENDIX.

The Clarence River Fresh Fish and Canning Company (Limited).

THE following particulars respecting this company have been supplied by Mr. Frederick A. Rankin, one of the promoters:—

In the early part of the year 1888 it was determined to test practically the question whether Australian fish could be profitably preserved after the style of English fresh herrings. Accordingly, in conjunction with my partner, Mr. E. J. M'Donald, I initiated arrangements at Iluka, a village at the Clarence River Heads. This venture subsequently merged into the Clarence River Fresh Fish and Canning Company (Limited). The fish treated consisted of whiting, sea-bream, black-bream, sea-mullet, and flat-tail mullet. As ours was the first attempt to place Australian preserved fish on the market, we had of course to contend with all such difficulties as those that usually beset the pioneers of a new industry. After repeated experiments we discovered that the only kinds of fish that could be profitably preserved were the mullet. All the other species commanded too high a price in the market in the fresh-caught state to admit of our company purchasing at a price which, for our purposes, would yield profitable results; indeed, it was only when there happened to be a glut of fish that we could get anything but mullet from the fishermen. Each basket of 80 lb. gross weight would average in the cans only from 42 lb. to 45 lb.

At the first start the demand for the article was so brisk that we found difficulty in providing the supply, but afterwards it began to slack off and finally ceased altogether. The reason of this was that our agents insisted upon our supplying them with cases of assorted kinds, to get which we had to employ boats for the purpose. This was quite outside the proposed objects of our company, and though it enabled us to provide the desired assortments, we could not produce them at a price to suit the public. Moreover, as the bream and other fish of hard-spined formation possess dense bone, which no amount of cooking will soften, we found that our treatment of those fish did not suit the popular taste. There was at one time a prejudice against the sea mullet, but that has been overcome, and fortunately so too, for when preserved in the proper season they really rival the tinned English salmon—certainly they are, for preserving purposes, the best fish in Australian waters. Our progress so far has proved that a good article can be turned out at a fair profit, but we have not yet fully completed arrangements for placing it properly upon the market. In this, however, we anticipate but little difficulty; but whether the business will ever become a large one will depend very much upon the possibility of being able to draw our fish supply from the sea. It is believed that this can be done, and in due time the company intends to make the experiment. Our industry seems capable of great developments, but as yet we have not advanced it beyond the embryo stage. The works of the company comprise in the canning department all the latest and best appliances, and by a small addition to the preserving department the company could, if required, turn out 4,000 1-lb. tins per diem. The company is also erecting cooling chambers for the storage of fish awaiting shipment in the fresh captured state to Sydney. For reasons already assigned, the immediate future operations of the company will be confined to mullet only. When the supply of whiting is in excess of the demand, all that can be obtained will be treated after the style of English kippered herrings.

Fresh Water Fish Acclimatisation.

By JOHN GALE, Queanbeyan.

IN July, 1888, Mr. F. Campbell, J.P., of Yarralumla, Queanbeyan, and I, went from the latter town to Ballarat, Victoria, and obtained from the Acclimatisation Society there a number of young trout, English perch, and Russian carp. We were to have been supplied with about 1,000 trout, which were placed in a nursery pond awaiting our arrival; unfortunately, the day before reaching our destination it was discovered that the pond had been netted by poachers, and the greater part of the fish stolen. We were fortunate, under the circumstances, in obtaining over 300 trout. They were yearlings, measuring from 3 inches to 5 inches in length, and strong vigorous fish. They were of two varieties—the American brown trout and the English spotted trout. In addition to these, we had about eighty perch and about forty carp. We were furnished with tin cans of about 6 gallons capacity each—two for the trout, and one each for the perch and carp. For the purpose of aerating and agitating the water in the cans containing the trout —an essential matter so far as trout in travel are concerned—we were also provided with a pair of bellows with 3 or 4 feet of india-rubber tubing attached to the nozzle. From the Acclimatisation Society's ground, on the margin of Lake Windouree, to the Ballarat Railway Station is about 2 miles distant, and I conveyed them thither in a waggonette. My companion had been detained at Melbourne by sickness, and on this morning I was to meet him on the Ballarat Station, and proceed with our delicate freight to Melbourne. During the stay of about thirty minutes on the railway platform at Ballarat, the fish tanks were allowed to rest without being aerated— an almost fatal oversight—for when the train arrived from Melbourne with my friend, and I took him to see the fish, the trout were all on their backs. Fortunately a few minutes' use of the bellows and tubing brought them round, and from that moment till we reached our destination there was no cessation in the use of the bellows. We had, by the indulgence of the Secretary for Railways, Victoria (Mr. Labertouche), a large saloon carriage to our exclusive use, so that we had every facility for manipulation. At Melbourne we had to wait six hours for the through express to Sydney. The station-master there kindly placed our fish in charge of a porter, whose duty it became during that time to incessantly use the bellows. From Melbourne to Yass (New South Wales), a journey of about fourteen hours, we had a compartment of a railway carriage to our exclusive use. It was through the night, and my companion and I took watch and watch of three hours each, during which the bellows were not permitted to be at rest more than ten minutes at a time. Till we reached Yass we had lost but one fish— a trout. Thence we had a special coach to carry us to Queanbeyan, a distance of 45 miles. At Jeir, about 20 miles from Yass, we diluted the water with some fresh from a small stream. There had been only one change before this, at Albury, water from the Murray River being substituted for that obtained from Windouree Lake. I feared the consequences, as the water was not only at freezing point, needles of ice being on the surface of the stream, but it tasted a little brackish. I, however, yielded to my friend's wish. Shortly after the mistake was evident, for the fish began to die—trout, carp, and perch. At Canberra, about 12 miles from our destination, we had upwards of forty dead fish. At this point Mr. Campbell was met by his servant man, to whom we entrusted about sixty trout, to be placed in the Cotter River (about 25 miles distant), a tributary of the Murrumbidgee fed by the springs from the Australian Alps—a magnificent stream for trout. We placed forty in the Queanbeyan River, sixty in the Molonglo River, twelve in the Yass River, and twelve in the Naas River, also tributaries of the Murrumbidgee, the same day. The balance we forwarded by coach and rail to Braidwood (34 miles) for the Little River, which flows seaward, and to Bibbenluke, Monaro, a tributary of the Snowy River. All these fish reached their destination without a single death. As an experiment, we also brought four trout, three perch, and three carp, in hermetically sealed jars, and the result was successful, only one trout—a little fellow sick from the start—succumbed. The distance from Ballarat to Queanbeyan is about 450 miles, and the fish were thirty hours in transit. Bibbenluke is another 100 miles, and Braidwood 34 miles; so that our efforts, so far as placing the fish in the waters of their respective destinations, were highly successful.

Not less so has been the result. We have no account from the Yass, Naas, or Little Rivers, but both in the Queanbeyan and Molonglo Rivers they have bred marvellously and grown large, having been occasionally caught as heavy as from 3 lb. to 5¼ lb. a year ago. The Cotter River is teeming with trout, and they are descending the Murrumbidgee River, having been caught at Cavan, near Yass. Mr. Edwards, to whom we entrusted those destined for the Bibbenluke River, the second year after the parent fish were placed there, netted hundreds of small trout by way of experiment.

My own opinion is, that your Department would meet with equal success, if instead of sending fry of only a month or two old, you could keep these in a nursery till at least a year old, and then distribute them.

Ours was the first successful effort that I know of of the introduction of trout into the rivers of New South Wales.

The perch and carp were all placed in waters near Queanbeyan, but I have heard nothing of them since.

The Correlation of the Inlets and the Offing Fisheries.

By Alexander Oliver, M.A.

In a letter published a few days ago I promised to say something on a subject not very accurately indicated by the heading to this letter. In redeeming that promise I should at the outset admit that anything like scientific elaboration of this most interesting question will not be attempted. Nevertheless, I am not without hope that some of the conclusions to which I have been brought may possibly induce a few thoughtful persons who take an interest in our sea fisheries to regard our inlet nurseries from a new point of view. We are told that we have nearly 700 miles of coast-line, lying between the 29th and 36th parallels of south latitude (Point Danger and Cape Howe). I believe the actual length of our coast-line measured along its margin must be at least 100 miles longer;

but let us take the official figures, and suppose our seaboard for purposes of the fisheries to be 680 miles in length. That seaboard is indented by large bays like Twofold, Jervis, Port Stephens, and Botany, and by an almost incredible number of inlets, the sea outlets of lagoons or lakes, varying in area from 100 to 100,000 acres. Add to these the embouchures of a large number of rivers and creeks springing from the main range or its foot-hills, and we have a vast and varied series of fish nurseries distributed along the entire length of our coast-line, the importance of which to the support of a constant stream of supply of the very best form of our food fishes has never yet been properly represented. Nor has the correlative value of these inlets to the migratory and other families of our sea fishes been, so far as I know, presented in its proper light. Between the coast-line and the 100-fathom line various intermediate lines of soundings have been taken, but no banks of any extent, I may say no true banks at all have been discovered. Deep soundings seem, as a rule, to approach every considerable promontory or high land along the whole length of our coast-line, and to recede eastward between the headlands of all bights. There are almost innumerable sunken rocks, known as "Bunboras," and large areas of foul ground, haunted by all varieties of rock-loving fish, particularly by the schnapper, the kingfish, and the traglin. There are islands, and islets, and rocks-awash in large variety, and there are the submarine continuations of rocky formations jutting out (below the sea level) for several, sometimes so far as 10 or 15 miles from land. In short, the offings afford all the variety of sea-bottom suitable as feeding grounds for our special forms of bottom fish, and among these for the schnapper, a fish which in our waters may, for economic purpose, stand for the cod of Northern Seas, just as the mullet, the most prolific of our high-swimming or surface fish, may be regarded as the substitute, for like purposes, of the herring of Northern Seas; but we must not fall into the prevalent error of assuming that our seas can ever afford such a harvest of schnapper or mullet as do the Northern Seas of Europe and America of cod and herring. The fact is that the possible "output" of schnapper is very limited compared with that of the cod family, and vast as are the schools of mullet, which from March to May in every year— sometimes as early as February—swarm out of every considerable river, lake, and inlet along the seaboard from the Gippsland Lakes to the Tweed River, that fish bears no comparison in the matter of fecundity with the clupeids, of which our "maray" is the Australian representative of the pilchard variety of that family.

True, we have never yet seriously attempted to gather in the harvest of our fisheries situated beyond half a day's sail from Port Jackson. Hundreds of square miles of the best of our grounds lie beyond the range of fishing-boat or railway, and many of these are still, to all practical purposes, virgin fisheries, and likely to remain so until steamers with cool chambers shall establish business relations between them and the metropolitan market. These virgin fisheries are, however, precisely the same as were the once famous grounds between Broken Bay and Port Hacking. They are stocked in exactly the same way as Long Reef and the Coogee offing grounds were once and might still be stocked, and a score of equally celebrated and productive grounds near Sydney which have satisfied our wants for more than half a century, but are now worked out. An examination of the Admiralty charts for those sections of the coast which lie northward of Terrigal and southward of Stanfield Bay, or, say Port Hacking, will best explain my meaning, if accompanied by a slight knowledge of the localities so much the better. The reader unprovided with charity will necessarily be at some disadvantage; and much that I have to say will have to be accepted by him, if at all, in faith. But he may be assured at all events on this point that what I shall ask him to believe will be derived from my own personal knowledge, acquired during a course of more than twenty years of coastal visitation, mostly out of the track of the intercolonial steamer, the timber ketch, and the newspaper reporter concerning the offing fisheries of the Colony. Then, I submit for the consideration of those who know, or care to know, something about their origin, and their prospects, as sources of supply for a large market, this proposition: The capability of any given schnapper ground, wherever situated on our coast, is measurable by its proximity to one or more inlets possessing tolerably deep and quiet waters, and not liable to be scoured by floods, or to have their salt-water converted into brackish by the contributions of rivers having their rise in the main range. It must, of course, be understood that this proposition has reference exclusively to the schnapper. The perches, the mullets, the flathead, the jew fish, the tailor, the black fish, and other forms of our edible fishes, have no antipathy to brackish water, but the schnapper in every stage of growth avoids it as if it were a poisonous environment. The occurrence of a flood in the Hawkesbury regularly means the exodus of the red bream, not only from the river and its embrochure, but for such a distance therefrom as may bring them to water of the necessary salinity. This statement may seem strange to those who know that flood-water, owing to its smaller specific gravity, floats over the salter water into which it is introduced, but the fact is, nevertheless, as I state it; and what is true of the Hawkesbury is true of the Tweed, the Clarence, the Richmond, the Macleay, the Shoalhaven, and the Clyde; that is to say, of all our rivers which bring down considerable volumes of fresh water from mountain or tableland sources. At this moment the volume of flood-water still coming down the Hawkesbury is such as to colour the water as far as South Head, three miles from the river's southern headland (Baranjo'). Few of the schnapper family can be found within the influence of their fresh water. There are, of course, red bream to be caught in the saline depths of Pittwater and Cowan and in the Broadwater of Brisbane Water, but whenever the fresh water makes its influence felt there very few of the speridæ (the schnapper family) will be found. The Hawkesbury water ceases to be discoloured by fresh water about the neighbourhood of Little Reef, about 5 miles from Baranjo, and the southerly current cleanses it in the offing, about three miles to the eastward of that promontory. Within these limits no schnapper will be found, or but very rarely. I have been informed, on the best authority, that precisely the same condition of things prevails on grounds within the influence of other rivers similar to the Hawkesbury; and I have no doubt that all along the coast-line the schnapper family have been evicted from their holdings in the neighbourhood of the rivers carrying mud-fresh water, and have been compelled to seek salter water away out to seaward. They will return, of course, to their accustomed haunts as the flood-waters are absorbed by the ocean or evaporated, but not before.

Returning now to my contention (that the capabilities of any given schnapper ground off the coast are measurable by its proximity to a commensurate area of deep and undisturbed salt-water inlet), I should like to guard myself from being misunderstood. I know perfectly well what magnificent catches of schnapper could at this moment be secured at scores of places far distant from any such inlets as I have described. For example, over the large area of foul ground marked by the Solitaries, off the Point Danger cluster of reefs, the Mermaid, Bumbora, and scores of other places.

It is certainly the fact that three fishermen, in ordinary weather, could easily fill a schnapper boat in a few hours. But these fisheries would never stand the racket of half a century's persistent fishing, as did Long Reef and the Port Hacking, Botany, Coogee, and Broken Bay grounds, as well as the grounds off our own harbour. In my opinion, a very few years' heavy fishing would impoverish them, because, unlike the grounds just mentioned, there are no neighbouring nurseries like Port Jackson, Cowan, Pittwater, Brisbane Water, Port Hacking, Botany, and George's River, from which they could draw constant streams of immigrating red bream. And though the coastal rivers are admirably conditioned for the propagation and growth of the mullet and other families, they are not for the schnapper family. There is too much fresh water in them in flood times, and in drought times they are too much infested by submarine growths fatal both to oyster life and to the lives of the young of some of the deep water fishes, of the schnapper family in particular.

With regard to the spawning of the schnapper, it is most unfortunate that very little is known. The commonly accepted belief among fishermen and other observers is that the schnapper spawns in quiet places outside the inlets as a rule, while some river-hunting fish spawn in suitable places within their range of habitat. The school fish, easily recognised by all of us who are familiar with the family, by their colour and other well-known features, are generally said to deposit their ova towards the middle of the summer months; as a rule, not later than February. The schnapper in its later developments is known to change its habitat, and to frequent inshore reefs and inlets, and there to spawn. The young fry in all cases seek for an asylum from their enemies, and for food otherwise denied them, in sheltered deeps where they can fatten on the spawn of other fish, and particularly of oysters and other mollusks and crustaceans, and on the manifold microscopic organisms in which the waters of these asylums are so fertile.

In shallow rivers, like those I have named, the black-bream and its congener the tarwhine prospers, but not the red bream. The red bream—that is to say, the year old progeny of the schnapper, generally hatched at sea, becomes from its cock-schnapper period, a denizen of the inlets. He is very rarely caught in the offing grounds. The inlets with deep water in them are his ordained nurseries, and in them he remains until, by an instinct not at present to be analysed by our observers, he feels that it is time for him to leave the nursery, and reach out to the submarine and tumultuous world outside. Let those nurseries be harried by nets and other agencies of destruction, as Port Jackson, Port Hacking, Botany, and George's River, and the deep portions of Broken Bay have been harried, and their offshore fisheries will report at once a lack of schnapper. But still some youngsters are left in the nurseries, and these, in due course, instinctively seek the reefs and school grounds outside, and the race, for market purposes, is not absolutely extinguished. So, all our neighbouring schnapper grounds, still though to a very limited degree, produce some schnapper. The catalogue of a successful day's fishing reaches a dozen fish now, which twenty years ago reached 20 or even 40 dozen. But the breed is not extinct, because the nursery is always at hand, and some few parent fish are left to restock their natural fattening grounds.

For the next decade or so I think the magnificent area of shoal grounds (known as Sir John Young Banks) lying slightly within the Shoalhaven Bight, and the equally productive grounds lying between the Broughton Islands and Cape Hawke, replenished in one case by the deep adjacent inlets of Jervis Bay, and in the other by those of Port Stephens, will be found sufficiently well stocked with schnapper to withstand the severest drain on their resources; but, unless those adjacent inlets are saved from the annihilating, ceaseless net—not at present I confess, a very serious trouble—certainly their capabilities of supplying the offing grounds in their vicinity will be diminished, until those grounds, at present almost virgin, are reduced to the pitiable condition of Long Reef, Coogee, and other grounds in the vicinity of Port Jackson.

It must be within the knowledge of all fishermen, professional or amateur, of middle age, that less than twenty years ago they could easily take from 6 to 20 dozen large red bream in such fisheries as Port Hacking, Botany, our own harbour, Pitt Water, or Brisbane Water in a morning's fishing. The catch would now be at most one or two fish for the dozen of that time. Of course the reason of this decadence is that the destruction of the younger generations is so large and so persistent that the offing fisheries have long ceased to receive their regular succession of two and three year old bream. The number of spawning fish on the outside grounds is therefore continually being diminished, while their enemies for the like reason increase. The leather-jacket—the worst enemy to the ova, and young fry of the schnapper—fills up the void caused by this systematic destruction and very largely augments it. Off any of the depths from Pelican and Belmont up to Cockle Creek in Lake Macquarie there might be caught without much trouble from 10 to 20 dozen of fine squires during a morning's fishing. I have frequently caught that number myself in years gone by. The result of persistent netting by seines, and the sunken nets or trawls, of the beaches and even the deep waters of that lake, is that one can now hardly procure a good mess of line fish during a whole day's fishing. And the offing fisheries of the lake from off Redhead to Catherine Hill Bay have proportionately suffered. The destruction in the lake has reacted on the supply outside Tuggarah Lake, and its outside schnapper grounds, from Bird Island to Terrigal high land, (Point Upright) have suffered in an exactly similar way.

Schnapper are still to be obtained in boatloads at the Sir John Young Banks because Jervis Bay and the waters of the Shoalhaven are comparatively free from netters. But it is said that the netting in Lake Illawarra has already told on the schnapper grounds off the Five Islands and their vicinity.

Enough, perhaps, has been said to make it obvious to any person, though but very moderately acquainted with the habits of the schnapper family, that the true schnapper nurseries for the school grounds off the coast of this Colony are the deepwater inlets in their vicinity, and that a permanent succession of fish can only be ensured in cases where the annual catch is balanced by the arrivals of young stock. The apparent exceptions to this conclusion, as I have hinted at, are derived from fishing grounds that have never been subjected to the constant drain of the Sydney market. The question then arises, is it, or is it not, too late to restock our exhausted schnapper fisheries within the home division by closing for a sufficient period the neighbouring deepwater inlets, which "are known" to be nurseries of the young schnapper. For example: Cowan and perhaps a portion of Pitt Water for the Broken Bay grounds; Middle Harbour for the Port Jackson grounds; Tuggarah Lake for the Tuggarah grounds; and by vigorously enforcing the closure of Port Hacking for the Botany grounds. At present we close the upper waters of our river and inlet fisheries, and, as a rule, open the lower or deep portions. I think the converse experiment is certainly also worth trying; for if the grounds within 30 miles of the Heads were restored even to their condition of ten or fifteen years ago, it would be a great boon both to schnapper fishers and schnapper eaters—that is to say, to the entire community.

Commissioners of Fisheries for New South Wales, appointed under the Fisheries Act, 1881.

Hon. W. Macleay......... President.
Hon. W. B. Dalley ......
Hon. H. C. Dangar ...... } Appointed 19 April, 1881.
Hon. Geo. Thornton ...
Mr. Alex. Oliver ....

		Date of Appointment.
Hon. Richard Hill	*Vice* Hon. Geo. Thornton, resigned.....	5 April, 1882.
Mr. Geo. F. Want	,, Hon. W. B. Dalley, resigned	5 May, 1882.
Mr. John H. Geddes ...	,, Hon. H. C. Dangar, resigned	5 June, 1882.
Mr. F. J. Thomas	,, Mr. Alex. Oliver, resigned	18 October, 1882.
Dr. Jas. C. Cox	,, Hon. W. Macleay, resigned.........	18 October, 1882.
Mr. Jas. R. Hill	*Vice* Mr. John H. Geddes, resigned ...	3 January, 1885.
Mr. Alex. Oliver	,, Mr. Geo. F. Want, resigned	13 May, 1885.
Mr. S. H. Hyam	,, Mr. F. G. Thomas, resigned	11 June, 1886.
Dr. Jas. C. Cox	President, reappointed	20 October, 1887.
Dr. E. P. Ramsay	*Vice* Hon. Richard Hill, resigned.........	5 November, 1887.

Present Board of Commissioners.

Dr. Jas. C. Cox......... ..	President, reappointed from	20 October, 1887.
Mr. Jas. R. Hill	Reappointed from	3 January, 1885.
Hon. S. H. Hyam	Reappointed from	11 June, 1886.
Dr. E. P. Ramsay	Reappointed from	5 November, 1887.
Hon. W. R. Campbell...	*Vice* Mr. Alex. Oliver, resigned.	
	Appointed from	5 May, 1890.

NOTE.—Doctors Cox and Ramsay have again been reappointed in their respective positions for a further term of five years.

Extracts from Report on the Worm Disease affecting the Oysters on the Coast of New South Wales.

BY THOMAS WHITELEGGE.

The Infected Area.—Hunter River.

THIS is very generally distributed, having been met with in various situations, from about half-tide line to moderately deep water, still the principal home of the worm appears to be on the mud flats above low-water mark. The oysters from this region were invariably infected with the worm, particularly those which lay loose on the surface or partially buried in the mud. Whilst those oysters which were fixed to some solid substance, and elevated ever so little above the surface of the mud were comparatively free from the pest.

From what I ascertained of the habits of the worm, it appears that a large amount of mud is necessary to its existence, and that the more muddy the place the better the worm thrives; such being the case, it is reasonable to suppose that those oysters which are fixed on some solid body, and somewhat above the surface of the mud, will have a better chance of escaping the ravages of the worm, than those which are partially buried in mud or lying loose on the surface. I conclude, therefore, that if some loose material, such as stones, old shells, &c., was placed on the mud-flats for the spat to set upon, removing it from direct contact with the mud, that the prevalence of the worm would be considerably diminished. In the absence of such material the worms have no other alternative but to fix on the oysters as a place of refuge.

Symptoms of the Disease.

Oysters which are badly infested with worms may be detected at a glance by their thick rounded outline, and the absence of thin sharp edges. Moreover, by looking along the anterior margins of the valves, the entrances to the worm tubes will, on close inspection, be readily seen; those openings furthest removed from the edges of the shell having a *keyhole-like outline*, whist those on the actual margins are *semicircular*. In the majority of cases the worms are found on the anterior margins of both the upper and lower valves, and frequently on the posterior margins, but rarely on other parts. On opening the diseased oyster, the valves will be seen to possess a series of blister-like structures, which are very variable in shape and extent, usually they are more evident on the lower valve than on the upper. On pressing the surface of these blisters with the point of a knife, it readily yields, and underneath will be seen a quantity of light brown mud in which the worms are embedded. Each worm has its own collection of mud, and from it a membranous tube often extends a short distance beyond the edge of the shell. The tube is invariably curved, but it is usually curved in such a way that the entrance and the outlet are in close proximity to each other, the inlet and outlet being often enclosed by the thin layer of shell deposited by the oyster. When viewed in section the opening of the tube is semicircular, the older part of the shell forming the base, and the newer layer the half-circle; or there are two openings, each consisting of three-fourths of a circle, with a space connecting them together, and bounded above and below by linear layers of shell. On removing the thin shelly matter it will be seen that the inner surface retains all the inequalities of the mud over which it was deposited, and forms a sort of mould of the inclosed mud, and rarely exhibits any distinct groove except near the edge. The older parts of the valves upon which the worm rests, exhibit grooves of certain depths, varying according to the length of time the worm has been in the shell. The grooves are deepest near the edges, and gradually get shallower inwards. During my observations I found about twenty examples in which very young worms had just entered the shells, and in all these cases the worms were surrounded by large patches of mud, and a thin membranous covering deposited by the oyster. On the removal of this mud, the surface of the old shell was quite smooth, without any trace of a groove—a lens when applied to the spot failing to show any erosion. The only means by which the place occupied by the worm could be detected was by the presence of the edges of the thin membrane formed by the oyster. The above-mentioned facts have an important bearing on the question as to how the worm gets into the shell, which is a much simpler process than has hitherto been supposed, inasmuch that it does not entail any far-fetched theories about the worm boring into the shell, with the assistance of an acid secretion from the body, or mechanically by means of its bristles. My opinion is that the worm does not bore into the substance of the shell at all, in the strict sense of the word.

How the Worms effect an entrance into the Oysters.

Before entering into details it will be necessary to take into consideration the habits of the young worm, which will, when fully stated, show that the boring theory is out of the question; and, further, that sections of the shell, if carefully examined, furnish sufficient evidence to show that all the appearances presented may be accounted for without supposing that the worm deliberately drills an opening into the solid shell. On the third day after my arrival at Newcastle, I found several clusters of ova, which I concluded were those of the *Polydora ciliata*. They were found on the sides of the membranous tubes of the worm, in little transparent sacs, each cluster somewhat less in diameter than the body of the worm, and each sac containing between fifty and sixty eggs. I placed some of these egg-sacs in a test tube and kept them for six days, during which time most of the eggs hatched out. On examining a cluster under the microscope, I observed the newly-hatched larvæ swimming about in the egg-bag, and by means of a dissecting needle, I ruptured the wall and allowed them to escape. They swim very rapidly by means of the oral and anal wreathes of ciliæ and the tufts of long stiff setæ, which they only used occasionally. They appear to jump or skip when the bristles are brought into play, and are consequently very difficult to follow under the microscope. At birth the body is about twice as long as broad, and consists of six segments. The antennæ are represented by small rounded lobes, the eyes are four in number, two near the mesial line, and two a little further forward and widely separated. On each side of the body there are a series of bristles, on the first segment there are about nine on each side, on the remaining segments the bristles diminish in size and number posteriorly.

For the first six days the larvæ swim about vigourously, after which they begin to settle down, and appear to be in search of some suitable place to commence life in earnest. At this stage it is very difficult to transfer them from one vessel to another by means of the dipping tube, from the fact that the moment they feel the current of water, they suddenly fix themselves on the sides of the tube, and no amount of shaking will move them. They hold on to the glass by the head with leech-like tenacity, whilst the rest of the body moves up and down with the water. The only way to get them on to a glass slide is to wait until they settle down to the bottom of the tube. This peculiar habit of being able to fix on an object suddenly, when caught in a current of water, is a very important factor in enabling the worm to select any spot it chooses for its abode. If the place first chosen is not convenient, it can move to another more favourably situated, even in the face of a strong current of water.

From what I have seen of the habits of the young worm in its free swimming state, and also of those already mentioned as having just settled down, I am of opinion that the young worm simply swims into the open oyster, and fixes itself by its head on the margin of the shell. If the position is suitable it immediately begins to construct a tube and collect a large quantity of mud. It may possibly be guided to the most favourable spot by the current of water drawn in by the oyster. If so, then we have the explanation why it is that the anterior margin is more often infested than any other part of the shell. The worms appear to have the power of collecting a large quantity of mud in a very short time. Some which I kept in confinement in moderately clear water added fully one-quarter of an inch to the length of their tubes in about an hour, and I have frequently removed the projecting tubes at night, and in the morning they have been repaired and projected beyond the edges of the shell fully half an inch ; so that a vigorous young worm on entering an oyster can soon accumulate a large quantity of mud, which is immediately covered over by the oyster with a thin layer of shelly matter, and if the oyster is healthy, the deposit is laid down quickly, confining the worm with its patch of mud to a very small space. On the other hand, if the oyster is unhealthy and already infested, the shelly deposition is slower and the worm collects a large patch of mud before the layer is solidified. Hence it is that the size of these accumulations of mud get larger as the worms increase and the oyster gets weaker. In some very severe cases the whole of the lower valves were covered with freshly collected mud, and the oysters were reduced to a mere skin, and utterly incapable of secreting any shelly matter. The effect of these blister-like structures, which increase in number and size as the disease progresses, is to practically fill up the whole of the lower valve and to bulge out the upper, so that there is no room left for the oyster.

In all cases the recently collected mud is of a light brown colour, and was found to be the work of young worms varying in length from one-eighth to half an inch, the patches of mud on the larger examples varying from one to one and a half inch in length, by one-half to three-quarters of an inch wide. In most of the examples mentioned the surface of the mud was covered by a thin pliable membrane. The mud surrounding the adult worm is usually more compact and darker in tint, often inclining to slate colour; whilst the mud which the worms have left is frequently black. No doubt it is partly due to the decomposition of this black mud that so many oysters die. The parts of the oysters overylying these putrefying patches are always discoloured by yellowish spots.

When the habits of the young worm are considered in connection with the evidence derived from the examination of oysters, in which the worm has just established itself, it points to the conclusion that the larvæ simply swim into the open shell; and there is no evidence of any boring having taken place, from the fact that the place occupied by the worm is quite smooth, and even in those cases in which the worm is full grown, the surface is often devoid of any grooves. It is only in old-established cases that grooves and tubular openings are found, and there they only exist on the margins as a rule. The above remarks apply to the old or thick parts of the valves; the newer thin deposit over the mud, as before mentioned, merely exhibits the irregularities of the surface over which it is laid whilst in a soft pliable condition, and is usually without any trace of grooves, except near the margin. Even these grooves, when examined with a lens, show a mould of what was beneath, without exhibiting any signs of having been bored. Another feature is the entire cavity occupied by the mud and worm, which cannot be accounted for by the boring theory. If the worm bores into the substance of the shell how are blister-like cavities formed? It is not reasonable to suppose that the worm has the power of raising a rigid layer of shelly matter and forming a blister. To do this the layer must be rendered pliable, otherwise there would be evidence of such raising in the shape of cracks, &c. If the blisters are formed by the disintegration of the shell, there ought to be some evidence on the inner surfaces; but there is nothing to show that disintegration had taken place. One surface is comparatively smooth, and the other a perfect mould of the enclosed mud.

Is is not more reasonable to suppose that the upper layer is deposited over the mud whilst in a soft state, simply covering the mud and worms, than to suppose that the worm bores into the shell and then forms the blister? If the blisters were formed by the disintegration of the shell, there ought to be some variation in the thickness of the layer, inasmuch as the disintegration would be unequal, and be most evident immediately over the worm. Such, however, is not the case; the deposited layer is pretty uniform in thickness over each blister.

The death of the oyster is brought about chiefly by the decomposition of the mud after the death of the worms; but no doubt the imperfect closing of the valves has its effect. In all cases in which the worms are numerous, the edges of the valves are defective, from the fact that the worms occupy the edge, and that the shelly deposits are used in lining the shell. Oysters that are infested with worms are much more sensitive than those which are free from them—at least those which I kept under observation were so. If the vessel containing them were disturbed, the diseased oysters were the first to close and the last to open. The sensitiveness will tend to deprive them of a large quantity of food. In addition there are the worms placed in the current which carries the food to the oyster, and which in bad cases may number from twenty to thirty, each feeding on the food drawn from the supply of the oyster.

Evidence as to Boring, from an examination of the Shell.

One frequent appearance of the interior of the valves tells very forcibly against the boring theory. In many cases the worm occupies an elevated position in the shell, projecting above its surface as much as half an inch. The heap of mud surrounding such worms is covered by a thin layer of shelly matter, and both the entrance and the outlet to the worm-tube stand up at right angles to the oyster-shell valve, so that the worm lives within the shell completely, and the ends of the tube have no connection with the outer water, except when the oyster is open. (See Plate 4, fig. 5.) Instances of this kind can only be explained by supposing that the worm and the mud have been enclosed by the shelly matter deposited by the oyster.

There appear to be three well marked stages in the appearance of sections of the shell when viewed from the outside and looking into the ends of the tubes. (See Plate 4, figs. 7, 8, 9.)

In the first stage we have the flattened solid part of the shell upon which the worm rests. Immediately over this is the thin layer formed by the oyster, which forms a semi-circular outline (fig. 7.) In this stage there are no grooves where the worm is in contact with the shell. In the second stage the basal surface is slightly grooved and the upper layer less of a semi-circle, and somewhat flattened (fig. 8). In the third stage the grooves are so sunken in the basal surface that they appear somewhat like a keyhole, and consist of two openings, each forming three-fourths of a circle, with a space connecting them together. It is the appearance presented in the third stage that has led to the idea that the worm bores into the shell. At first sight such openings certainly look as if they had been bored; but if the various stages are carfully examined, with due regard to the time the worm has been in the shell—which may be determined by the colour of the enclosed mud, the size of the worm, the thickness of the shelly deposit, and the condition of the surface upon which the worm rests—the different phases presented may be traced easily, and the only way to get at the facts is to follow up what are evidently the early stages of the disease. In the first place the worm swims into the open shell, and settling down on the surface, near the margin, it at once collects a quantity of mud. The oyster, the moment it feels the presence of a foreign body, begins to deposit a layer of shelly matter, which determines or limits the extent of the muddy patch, according to the rapidity with which it is laid down and solidified. At this stage the worm rests on a smooth surface, and is covered over by a thin layer of shell. The oyster still continues to deposit shelly matter, and the growth at the edge tends to force the opening occupied by the worm further out. The body of the worm, resting on the shell, has by reason of the constant movements in and out, a tendency to wear away the surface.

Whether this is accomplished by strictly mechanical means, or by a corrosive acid, I am unable to say; but the fact remains that it is worn away. If the worm has been long in the shell, the grooves formed are deep, and the longer they remain the deeper they become. When measured from the out-

H

side inwards they are longer and more tubular; but this is owing to the fact that the growth or increase in the size of the shell forces the entrances further outwards and upwards, or downwards, as the case may be, according to whether it is the upper or lower valve which is affected. Ultimately the openings have the keyhole-like aspect which look as if they had been bored, but which, if carefully examined, will show that they have passed through the various phases before mentioned, *becoming shallower inwards and ceasing to be grooved at all.*

The Remedy.

There are several ways in which to deal with the worms, with a view to their destruction. Those I experimented on in various ways during a period of two months, I have had under observation daily during the whole of that time. Some of the worst cases were placed in fresh water, which had the effect of killing the worms and some of the oysters; the latter were no doubt killed by the putrescent germs developed in the mud after the death of the worms. Others which were kept without water for fourteen days, were afterwards placed in salt water for several days, and in all cases the worms were destroyed, whilst the oysters appeared to be in a healthy condition. Some which were kept in an extempore aquarium for over two months, were cultivated until the whole of the worms had died out. This I attributed to the water supplied, not on account of its being bad, but from the fact that it was moderately clear and free from mud, which seems so essential to the life of the worm.

From the above series of experiments we may conclude that placing the oysters in fresh water for a few days will destroy the worms. But this method has its drawbacks from the difficulty of transporting them over long distances, and could only be used in favourable localities. The most effective as well as the quickest method would be the drying process. The oysters should be removed from the beds, freed from mud by washing, and then placed under a shed or cover of some kind, to protect them from the sun's rays. The oysters should be spread out in thin layers, and occasionally turned over, so as to ensure the thorough drying of the shells externally. The process may be continued for ten days or longer—if the oysters would stand it. They might afterwards be relaid on the beds, if suitable ground exists on which to lay them—that is to say ground having a stony or shelly bottom. If they are laid on a mud surface, they will very soon be infested again. Another method which might be useful would be to remove the oysters into prepared ponds, into which none but moderately clear water is allowed to enter, or place them on a sandy or pebbly beach in such a position that they would be exposed to the sun, and get partially dry between every rise and fall of the tide. No doubt if either course was adopted and continued for some months, the worms already in the oysters would be destroyed. The above mentioned remedies can only be applied to oysters that are loose or attached to small objects, such as shells, &c.

So long as oysters are cultivated on the bare surface of the mud, they will be liable to the attacks of the worm; but if some solid substratum be provided for the spat to fix upon, and so remove them from direct contact with the mud, the oysters will have a chance of escaping the disease.

As far as I can ascertain, nothing has yet been published in reference to the eggs of the worm, and the following, if new, may be of interest :—The ova appear to be matured in the body of the worm and commence on about the thirtieth segment. Each succeeding segment to about the fiftieth bears a pair of egg-sacs, each of which contains between fifty and sixty eggs. The egg-cases are deposited on the sides of the membranous tubes inhabited by the worm, and remain in this position until the young worms are hatched. (Fig. 10, plate 1). It appears to me that the brood-pouches are formed within the body of the worm, and at the period of deposition the outer circle is ruptured, and the egg-sacs fixed on the sides of the tube. Before the eggs are deposited, the body of the worm is plump and of a cream colour, with a central line varying in colour from bright red to a very dark brown. Afterwards the body appears thin and of a chocolate colour, and appears almost like another species. In fact until I carefully examined those which had laid their eggs, I thought there was a second species inhabiting the oysters. The period during which the worms produce ova may be stated to be the months of October, November, and December. How far the breeding extends beyond these months I am unable to say; but it probably is within the mark to say that it may extend for a month or six weeks on each side.

The worm does not seem to confine itself to the oyster; it is common in other bivalves in Port Jackson. Its distribution appears to be world-wide. It is found in Europe, North America, Australia, and the Philippine Islands. There is also a species described by Schmarda from the Chilian Coast of South America, which may prove to be the same.

The Oyster Fisheries Laws.

Address delivered before the Linnean Society, by the President, Dr. JAMES C. COX, 1883.

THE laws and regulations under which our oyster fisheries are at present worked are, I regret to say, very unsatisfactory, and much good may be accomplished by bringing this question frequently and prominently before the public, so that, by pointing out where and how the laws are defective, they may be amended. We had taken from our oyster-beds, from July, 1881, to July, 1882, over 65,000 bushels of oysters, leased, which paid a royalty of £1,823. That portion dredged from natural oyster-beds, not the other portion paying no royalty, is obtained at an insignificant price from old leases, which, I am glad to say, will expire during the present and next year. As this subject, it is to be hoped, is likely to receive the attention of our legislators during the present session of Parliament, it will not be out of place to take this opportunity of passing under review the laws relating to this important question. Up to the year 1868 any person was at liberty to collect or take oysters for private use, or for sale as a marketable product, from any part of our tidal waters in which they were found; but up to this date oysters were not only indiscriminately collected for the purposes of food, but were very extensively collected for the purpose of burning them to make lime. Since railway communication has been established we are supplied with marble lime from the interior; prior to this almost the whole of the lime used was obtained from the shell-fish of our coasts, and living oysters contributed principally to its production; the only other shell-fishes which contributed a noticeable share at all to the production of lime were what are known as our mud-cockle (*Anomalacardia Trapezia*, Desh.) and our mud-lark (*Potamides Ebeninum*, Brug.). I know of an instance where a contract was taken to supply 6,000 bushels of lime, in which the contractors openly acknowledged that every ounce of it was obtained from living oysters. This indiscriminate waste of so valuable an article of food attracted the notice of the authorities in 1868, which resulted in an Act being passed (31 Victoria, No. 20) "To regulate oyster fisheries and to encourage the formation of oyster-beds." Our natural oyster-beds had already exhibited signs of exhaustion, and that Act had for its object the prevention of this exhaustion and their threatened extinction. It had also in view the encouragement of the cultivation of artificial oyster-beds. and the improvement of those now known as natural beds. By this Act of 1868 persons were permitted to lease Crown lands covered and uncovered by the ebb and flow of the tide for any time not exceeding ten years, for the laying down or forming of oyster-beds; the lessee was not allowed to possess any exclusive right or title to the shore except for forming oyster-beds. By a regulation under this Act the lease was restricted to 1 mile of shore frontage, which was let by tender or by auction. This Act did not define how far out from his shore frontage the lessee was entitled to lay down oysters on artificial beds, and it did not prevent him from dredging and taking oysters from what we now define and know as natural oyster-beds on his lease; the Act was really misread, and the natural oyster-beds were leased and worked under it. Under this 1868 Act there were no licenses granted to persons to dredge oysters beyond the limits of the tidal lands taken up as frontage leases, as there are in the present Act; at that time the difference between a natural oyster-bed, which is never uncovered by the ebb and flow of the tide—and an artificial bed formed by oysters being removed from the rocks or foreshore, and laid down on beds which are freely washed by the tides, and where they would receive consequently more nourishment and thrive better—was not understood. The oysters forming the natural beds in our rivers, streams, bays, &c., differ so materially from those which attach themselves to the rocks or other objects on the foreshore, and are uncovered by each tide, that the present Act has made provision for the working of these two natural positions of our oysters quite distinctly. Up to about 1872 our oyster fisheries were carried on under the regulation I have mentioned, when it was represented that the 1-mile frontage system was not extensive enough to carry on dredging operations with profit, and the Executive decided to repeal it. By the repeal of this regulation it was left open to the Lands Department of the day to lease any extent of frontage, and, as a matter of fact, whole rivers were leased by tender or by auction to single individuals, without any reference as to natural or artificially laid down beds. To Mr. Lindsay Thompson is due the credit of having repeatedly pointed out that all these leases had been erroneously and illegally promised, and the possession of them was entered upon quite beyond the provisions of the Act. These repeated representations resulted in the appointment, in 1876, of the Royal Commission on Oyster Culture. This Commission, after taking extensive evidence, recommended the cancellation of these so-called leases, the substitution of a system of licensing, and the appointment of an efficient staff of inspectors. Appended to their Report was a Bill for regulating the oyster fisheries, which the Commission strongly recommended to be passed into law. Through Cabinet changes this Bill was never brought before Parliament. Mr. Farnell applied for and obtained leave to bring in his Bill, but before he was able to do so the Ministry of the day resigned office. Unfortunately, by this misadventure the working of these extensive river leases continued, with one or two exceptions, till the expiration of the period of their ten years' leases. One lessee had the monopoly of no less than three rivers at one time, and there was not at that time any restriction to the size of the oysters taken off the beds; it can easily be imagined how exhausted and denuded these beds became. No doubt the lessees, for their own interests, did lay down oysters very largely on the old natural oyster-beds, but they did not lay them down as they do now; they attempted, in fact, to replenish the natural oyster-beds composed of our drift oysters with the oysters clinging to the rocks and other objects on exposed tidal lands. The artificial laying down of oysters was not then carried on with the success which it is now, by removing oysters from the rocks or other parts of exposed tidal land and placing them in more favourable positions. This state of things continued until 1880, when a Commission was appointed to inquire into and report upon the actual state and prospects of the fisheries of the Colony, and on the Report of this Commission, so ably drawn up by the Hon. William Macleay, the Fisheries Act of 1881 became law. Under the 28th section of this 1881 Act any person can lease 25 acres of tidal waters for thirty years, the boundaries of which have to be marked by poles or buoys. The Act is indefinite as to the shape of these leases, though the regulations infer the boundary lines of leases should be at right angles to the tide, but the 25 acres so taken up must not include a natural oyster-bed, which means, "Any bank, bed, or place of deposit in any tidal waters wherein oysters which have not been laid down by artificial means are, or shall be, found; but excluding rocks, stones, mangroves, or other trees or dead timber, or any other substance above mean low water-mark whereon oysters are, or may be, found attached or growing." It gives permission to take up this acreage to any extent of shore frontage, provided that this shore frontage has not been alienated by the Crown; it does not restrict the lessee from going out any distance he chooses from the shore into any depth of water; the lessee may surround a natural oyster-bed, by his acreage, but he must not work it. Although persons may lease land below the mean line of low water-mark by this 29th section, for the purpose of forming oyster-beds or laying such, this right is somewhat obscured by the 7th subsection of the same, which says "that occupation under such lease shall not give any right or title to form oyster-beds nor layings on the shore, nor to occupy or use any portion thereof not included in his lease, except as prescribed by the regulations," of which there are none. I might explain here that the word "shore" is defined by the Act to mean the portion of Crown land situated between mean high and mean low water-marks; or, in other words, is that portion of tidal land commencing from a point midway between very high water-mark and ordinary high water-mark, and extending out to a greater or less distance to a point midway between very low water-mark and ordinary low water-mark. For this lease 5s. an acre is paid for the first four years, and 20s. an acre for the remainder of the time. Section 32 provides that if any person owns, leases, or occupies land bounded by tidal waters, he may take up the water opposite his land, commencing from between mean high water-mark and a line approximately parallel thereto, and extending out from the last-named point to a depth of 3 feet of water at low spring tide; the lessee or owner of such land can take up the whole water frontage opposite to his land outwards to the depth mentioned, by paying £1 a year for every 100 yards frontage or part thereof in length; he can only make use of this tidal water land for laying down oysters artificially on the natural surface of the shore, or forming artificial beds for oysters to grow on. The two forms of leasing mentioned refer only to Crown tidal lands on which oysters may be laid on natural surfaces, or on which oysters can be laid down on artificially made beds. A special law is provided to work the natural oyster-beds composed of drift oysters; they are not leased at all, but persons are licensed under the 36th section of the 1881 Act to dredge them, and the same license permits the holder to dredge abandoned artificial beds, or those even which have been withdrawn from lease. Such licenses are granted either for twelve months or for three months; for a yearly license £10 a year is paid, and for the quarterly £3. This fee authorises the holder and his servants, the crew of one oyster dredger, but how many the Act does not say, to dredge. Oysters are taken from a variety of depths by dredging—at Port Macquarie, 40 feet; at Port Stephens, 10 to 40 feet; in some places, such as the Clyde and George's Rivers, when the bottom is irregular and rocky, they are very successfully obtained by divers. All oysters which are dredged from natural oyster-beds by license have to pay a royalty at the rate of from 1s. 6d. to 4s., according to the river or bay from which they come, for every bag containing 3 bushels. As these natural oyster-beds would soon become exhausted if every oyster dredged were taken off, it became necessary to fix on a legal size. A standard measurement, ascertained by a ring $1\frac{3}{4}$ inches in diameter, is established, and any oyster which will pass through such a ring is not permitted to be taken, and must be returned to the bed; if 3-bushel bags of oysters are found to contain an unfair proportion of oysters below the standard diameter they are seized by the Crown and confiscated. This regulation applies generally to all oysters, whether taken from natural beds or off rocks or foreshore, or beds laid down or artificial beds. There is a fourth provision in which oysters *inter alia* can be cultivated under this 1881 Act. By Part 3 private oyster fisheries are permitted to be made in this way. If any person owns low-lying land in the vicinity of tidal waters, he may, by application to the Minister charged with the administration of this Act, get permission to dig a trench from the tidal water to his land, and let the water run in and cover it. It is only permitted to dig a trench 12 feet wide for this purpose, and it must be always properly bridged over. For this privilege, if granted, a license is issued to the applicant for him to work it, for which he pays £10. So says the introduction to the Act (see page 13), but it does not say if this license is to be renewed annually. Oysters taken to market from beds which have been laid down, or grown on artificial beds on the old leases which have not yet expired, do not pay a royalty as those do which have been dredged or taken from the natural beds. By some oversight, the oysters growing on the shore, which, as before stated, means the portions of the Crown lands situated between mean high and mean low-water mark, are not, except on the leased areas, protected by the Fisheries Act of 1881. Any person can take them off the shore, whether licensed or not, and sell them, provided they are of a legal marketable diameter. Such shore oysters are not even protected by closing the natural oyster beds in rivers or harbours, because natural oyster beds are defined to be situated 3 feet below low water-mark This is one of the many urgent reasons why amended legislation of the Fisheries Act should be obtained. A great uncertainty exists in the minds of the public as to the conservation of our shore rock oysters. I will briefly recapitulate the only way in which they can be protected. The Governor by notification in the *Gazette* can declare any portion of the shore abutting on tidal waters, and being the property of the Crown, to be exempt from leasing and an oyster reserve. (Reg. 35.) This will protect such parts of the shore whereon oysters grow, because the line of exemption begins at a point midway between very high tide and ordinary high tide, termed by the Act "mean high water." Unfortunately there is very little of such shore now left adjoining Government land. Persons owning private property abutting on tidal lands on which oysters grow, cannot stop any person (whether licensed or unlicensed) from taking off oysters, unless a lease be granted to them of the adjoining tidal land. Unfortunately many persons who own private properties, and who wish to conserve and protect the oysters on the tidal boundary of their property, find it no easy matter to get a lease of the adjoining tidal lands granted to them. This is not their fault, for they make the necessary application for such land; nor is it the fault of the Commissioners who have the administration of the law, but it is altogether owing to the portions of tidal land applied for not being so accurately surveyed as to have a plan or tracing endorsed on the lease defining the position and boundaries of the land intended to be leased sufficiently accurately to satisfy the Survey Department, and until this is done the Crown Law Office will not issue the lease; they cannot claim the oysters till their lease is granted. The result is that the shores of our harbours are getting literally denuded of oysters. The only course at present open to landowners to have the oysters protected growing on the tidal boundary of their properties is to apply to the Commissioners to have such land declared an oyster reserve, which permits the owners to take bottlesful of oysters off such reserve; but no one else. It is now about two years since the Act of 1881 was passed into law, and although the Act is clear on most points as to the manner in which the leases can be granted, it is a positive fact that not a single lease up to the present time has been issued to form or plant oyster beds or layings under any of the sections (28-32 and 48). Of course it is quite competent for those who hold leases of rivers under the old Act, and which have not yet expired, to lay down oysters in beds where they will fatten and grow, and until their old leases expire such layings are safely protected, but immediately their leases do expire, the river in which they are is closed, and, unless again opened by proclamation, are not open to any licensed oyster dredger. It really is from this source of laid down beds on leased rivers that this and other markets of the colonies are to a great extent supplied with oysters. Unless, therefore, new leases are granted under this 1881 Act, or some other provision be soon made to give other oyster capitalists time to lay down oyster beds which will be secured to them, a period must arrive when the only supply can be obtained by licensed dredgers from natural oyster beds, and which, if I am not very much mistaken, will yield a very inadequate supply for the demand now created. It has come to this, that no new leases are being issued and the old leases are rapidly falling in, and cannot as heretofore be renewed, and we can only depend on our natural drift oyster-beds for the supply required, It will very naturally be asked, why are not new oyster leases issued. There is no want of applications from men of capital and experience, who are ready and willing to go into the trade if they can only obtain secure leases. The Fisheries Commissioners recommend such leases should be granted, but still they are not, and for the reasons beforementioned. What then, under the circumstances, would be best to be done? For my own part, I see no other way of solving this difficulty and urgent want than by having all the clauses of the 1881 Act relating to the leases of our oyster beds repealed at once. It would take some years to have a survey so accurately made of our east coast rivers as to justify the Crown Law Office to issue leases, even if they had a staff to do the work, which they have not, and until then must we go without a supply of oysters. If these leasing clauses were repealed, a simple plan for leasing our river beds for the laying down and cultivation of oysters could be carried out as suggested by the Surveyor-General, provided that the Crown law would issue such leases without requiring a plan or tracing defining the area of such leased tidal lands to be drawn on the leases. The suggestion of the Surveyor-General is to this effect, that on each side of the banks of our rivers a surveyor who should be specially told off to look after this work, should fix definite points say at a mile distant from each other; that such blocks of tidal waters should be bounded on the shore side by high water-mark or some fixed distance from it, and on the opposite side by the centre of the river stream; that an oyster capitalist should have leased to him one or more of such mile wide blocks for a term say of 12 years. The revenue returns for such leases may be by auction or tender, or a royalty paid by the bushel on all oysters raised, and I confidently believe that this plan would yield a more lucrative revenue. Many of such blocks could be reserved for breeding purposes, others reserved for licensed dredgers; and the oysters fringing the shores, to a certain distance from high water-mark should, if on Crown lands, be kept as reserves, and when on private property be leased to the owners of the property for a nominal sum, which, if they did not avail themselves of, should be claimed by the Crown. The recent complete and overwhelming destruction of all our property involves us in a momentous struggle that will require our utmost energies and persistent action to overcome. Let us then act strenuously and unitedly for the great cause, until we regain step by step the prosperous condition we held as it were but yesterday.

The Australian Oyster, its Cultivation and Destruction.

By JAMES C. COX, M.D., F.L.S., President of the Fisheries Commission.

FOR some time past letters and articles have appeared in the press concerning the oysters of our coasts. All seem to agree on one point, that the supply of oysters is not now what it was in former years, either in quantity or quality, and is certainly not sufficient to meet present wants. Many correspondents account for this falling off in the supply by the fact that it has been permitted in past years, up to a very recent date, to take from the beds every oyster which could be gathered, by any possible method, without steps having been taken to replace the loss. Others, again, seem to think that the oysters have been attacked in recent times by diseases which they call the "worm" and the "mud disease," and in this way account for the decrease; and various suggestions have been made by experienced and intelligent oyster culturists, with regard to remedies which should be adopted for the recovery of our natural supplies. The last legislative enactment was passed to meet the desire of oyster culturists who wished to obtain long leases of our foreshores reaching from a point between high and low water mark to mid-channel of our estuaries along the coast from 100 to 2,000 yards in length. Since the Act was passed, a very large number of leases has been issued, securing what, in the opinion of our oyster culturists are the places most suitable for their purpose. This process has been one purely of free selection, allowing them to exercise their own judgment as to the best foreshores on which to carry on their hopeful industry.

I cannot say that we can congratulate ourselves on the results, so far, which have been attained by this enactment. Oyster culturists have endeavoured to stock their selections by taking, with permission, oysters from the rocks and shallow foreshores of other parts of the coast which have not been leased, and have laid these oysters down in varying positions similar to those from which they were taken, and in varying depths of water—even, in some instances in great depths. Others have taken the recently-formed seed oysters adhering to cobbler's pegs, mangroves, whelks, twigs of dead branches of trees situated within tidal influence, and small broken pieces of stone; and have placed these in the positions which they considered the best for inducing them to mature, or in positions where by experience they know oysters had thriven well in past years, before the ruthless wholesale removal of them was carried on by dredging. As a rule, these oyster culturists have met with disappointment, although I do not believe our oyster beds are in the impoverished conditions which the public is generally led to suppose them to be. A few far-seeing of the number have steadily been acquiring very large leased areas; and these few have, it appears to me, been quietly stocking their newly-acquired leases, without disturbing them by wishing to get a rapid return for an important investment. That a large return will in very many instances be the result of this prudent forethought I have no doubt. On the other hand, I regret to say that there have been many cases in which well-stocked shores have been taken up with no other object than to denude those shores of every oyster which existed on them, and not with the intention of improving them. No doubt, even the most intelligent of our oyster culturists have met with very serious disappointment in their investments; and I attribute their want of success to several causes which they have not sufficiently thought about. One of these is that they expect that the seed oysters which they obtained from between high and low-water mark (*ostreæ cucullatæ*, or rock oysters) will produce *ostreæ subtrigonæ*, or drift oysters if placed on beds on which we know drift oysters once throve in abundance. I have, myself, always considered that these two kinds of oysters are different; but other conchologists have differed from me in this opinion, and believe that our rock oyster and our drift oyster are one and the same mollusc found under different conditions in greater depth of water.

Our mud oyster seems to have been absolutely ignored by our oyster culturists in their endeavours to cultivate the mollusc as an article of food. It is strange that this mud oyster, which only differs in a very slight degree in the form of its shell from the oyster (*ostrea edulis*) which supplies the European markets, should have been so ignored by them. The slight differences in its shell have induced conchologists to recognise it by another scientific name (*ostrea angasi*), for purposes of identification; otherwise it is undoubtedly the same mollusc which supplies the European markets; and a variety of which is the oyster with which the markets of the United States are principally supplied. There this variety of it is known—also for purposes of identification—as *ostrea borealis*. A variety of the same oyster, in the opinion of no less an authority than Professor Hutton, exists on the New Zealand coast, and threatens to become a formidable opponent to our New South Wales oyster. I am quite sure that were our mud oyster cultivated and educated as it is now in Europe, it would be brought to the same perfection as the European and American oyster. The cry is that it will not keep and will not carry. The same was said of the European oyster until its cultivators came to discover that by a gradual process of raising, it might be educated to keep quite long enough for all commercial purposes. I have myself tried many experiments with this oyster; and I have satisfied myself that it will live out of the water certainly from ten days to a fortnight if educated to do so. It is owing to the known habits of this species, as it appears in the United States waters, especially as reported upon in the United States Commission of Fish and Fisheries of 1880, that some of our oyster culturists have jumped to the conclusion that our drift oyster and our rock oyster are not replenished by seed oysters from our estuaries and rivers, but from beds of oysters which exist in the open sea, the spawn of which is floated into these places. If this opinion is attempted to be relied upon, and acted on practically, I predict that very serious disappointment will follow. I believe that our fine mud oyster, so much ignored, does exist outside the heads of our harbours, just as they do in Europe, in America, and in New Zealand, and even in Victoria, South Australia, and elsewhere. But what use is it discovering their whereabouts as long as this splendid oyster is neglected and ignored?

The spawn of the oyster similar to our mud oyster in Europe and in America is not a surface floating spawn; and, from the experiments I have made with ova taken from our mud oyster, I am satisfied also that it is not a surface swimming spawn. Let me mention that there was a time when this oyster was so abundant (as is evident from the remains of its shells in the old camp-ovens of the native tribes of this coast, and from the deposit along our muddy shores) that it was the only oyster which the natives thought worthy of carrying to their haunts to cook. If we may judge from these evidences, they must have existed in enormous numbers, as abundant as they are found at the present day in most of the undisturbed lakes between Shoalhaven and Eden, where, in one lake, I am informed, they exist in hundreds of tons. If this mud oyster exists outside our harbours, and produces its kind in our lakes and rivers, it will be said why should there not be beds of our drift oysters also outside our harbours, the spat of which, like the spat of the mud oyster, would be carried into our estuaries, and come to maturity on their own selected ground? All I can say is that, having endeavoured to examine the nature of the spawn of the drift oyster, I have reason to believe that its ova are heavy and unsuited for being floated far and wide, and that it adheres to any object close to which it was extruded from the ripe oyster. Notice how genuine drift oysters when taken from their natural bed are adhering to small fragments of shell or gravel which is found on the bed. Such oysters are always found on circumscribed beds. You do not find them generally disseminated over the bottom of the estuary, where they grow. If a pile be driven down on a bed of these oysters you will not find the young adhering to it from the surface of the bed to the point above high and low water mark. But at the latter point you will find not drift oysters adhering, but oysters similar to our common rock oysters. Again, if this oyster were the same species as our common rock oyster we would naturally expect to find it growing to the whole rocky surface of the bank where it exists from the bottom up to the zone, where we find our rock oysters exist. But this is not the case. There is an intervening gap between these two kinds free of oysters altogether.

Until recently I have been under the impression that our drift oyster did not adhere along its whole under surface to fixed objects such as rocks. But in this I now feel sure that I was mistaken; for divers have brought up from 70 to 80 feet deep, and even from greater depths, undoubted specimens of our drift oyster adhering throughout almost the whole of the under surface, from localities where beds of drift oysters were once abundant in a loose state, but which had, by dredging, almost all disappeared; these adherent oysters had escaped the dredge. I think, therefore, that sufficient attention has not been devoted to the replenishment of our natural beds with their own kind.

I have never myself succeeded in making rock oysters grow or live beyond a very limited period by sinking them in cages many feet below where they are naturally found. Recently attempts have been made to establish oysters on what were known as old drift oyster-beds, by depositing on them rock oysters imported from New Zealand. This experiment has proved as unsuccessful as the laying down on such beds of our own rock oysters. My theory is that our drift oysters, our mud oysters, and our rock oysters, require their own special food. Now, this is the real point on which I think all oyster-culture has failed in these waters. It is now an established fact that the *ostrea edulis* of Europe, its variety *ostrea borealis* of the waters of New York, its variety *ostrea angasi* of this coast, and the variety of *ostrea edulis*, which also occurs on the New Zealand coast, all require a diatomatic food for their existence. Other foods, no doubt, are consumed by these oysters, such as the embryo forms of other molluscs, hydroids, bryozoa, the larval forms of rhizopods and crustacean, and minute zoospores; but living diatoms form the principal element of their food. I have strong reasons for saying that our drift oysters are dependent on a similar class of food for their existence. I have not been able to convince myself that our rock oysters are dependent on living diatoms for their existence. On the contrary, the quantity of diatomatic *debris* extruded from them is remarkably small. Their position appears to me to be well suited to enable them to live on the larval forms of those classes which I have mentioned as forming part of the mud oyster's food. If I am correct in my observations, this will go very far to establish the fact that these rock oysters are not of the same species as our drift oysters.

Now, let me point out how this neglect of the study of the food of our oysters has been the means of preventing oyster-culturists from being successful in establishing new beds of oysters on ground which, to all appearances, was well suited to the purpose; but fresh water did not exist there, and diatomatic life depends for its existence, to a great extent, on the presence of fresh water. That intelligent observer, Mr. Woodward, has almost come to the same conclusion as myself without knowing the reason why, and has told the public that oyster life depends on the salinity of the water. In former days, when our mud and drift oyster-beds were in their prime, the land on each side of our estuaries and inlets running up into our rivers and creeks was thickly timbered and untilled. On the banks of many of these estuaries were situated pools of naturally-preserved fresh water—in fact, in some instances, extensive lakes. Such reservoirs of fresh water have been got rid of by removing the timber, thus allowing of evaporation, and by draining them into the sea. Now, these reservoirs have really been the source from which the diatomatic food of the oyster has been derived. Formerly the water was conducted by some subterranean means into the bottom of the estuaries of the sea, and there welled up; and it was around these subaqueous springs of fresh water that the oysters developed in beds, and throve so well. While influences have been at work to destroy this source of diatomatic water supply, other influences have been at work to assist the now starved-out oysters in dying off from their beds. The ground which was recovered by clearing and drainage has been ploughed up for agricultural purposes. The loose earth on the surface so ploughed up has been washed into these estuaries, and has in many instances suffocated, as it were, the oysters in their natural position. Such estuaries and rivers are continually being stirred up by the screws and paddles of our steamships. The water which flows over the oysters is constantly in a state of disturbance. The stirred-up mud gets into their gills, and the animals have not power to expel it. They have attempted to combat its offensive presence by throwing out a nacreous shelly covering, which alarmists tell you is a new disease among our oysters. This process of mud choking has not only occurred to oysters, but also to all bivalves, as is too evidently seen in the destruction which has taken place in the beautiful *trigonias* of our harbour, and in the large handsome-frilled Venus which once existed in such profusion in the Parramatta River, but which now, like our drift and mud oysters, has been almost absolutely wiped out, although it has never been used as an article of food.

In support of my theory that the destruction of our bed oysters is caused by the two influences which I have mentioned, and others which I could give, I make the following quotations from "The Food of the Oyster; its Conditions and Variations"—by Mr. Bashford Dean, A.B., published in the supplement to the Second Report of the Oyster Investigation and of Survey of Oyster Territory of the State of New York for the years 1885 and 1886 :—

"Water was collected from several beds selected and examined forty-eight hours after it was taken. The food of the oyster, together with its conditions and variations, was noted in each specimen. Not only was the quality of the food of the oyster examined, but also the proportions of the different kinds of minute plants and animals of which it was composed. The end in view was to ascertain the variation in the amount of oyster food, and the abundance or scarcity of the microscopic life which controls the condition of the oyster; the effect of season, weather, temperature, and general condition of the water as affecting the oyster and its food. This essential information regarding the most favourable conditions for oyster cultivation, all of which would be of value to the planter in selecting and managing his oyster grounds, had heretofore been scarcely touched upon. All work in the direction of increasing the supply of oysters must include information regarding its living. Much as we owe to Dr. Brooks, Professor Ryder, and Professor Rice for their researches in regard to the life history and embryology, much farther investigation will be required before its hygiene can be understood ; for even the oyster may have its conditions of welfare dependent upon food, weather, and locality."

"What we want to know is the principal local varieties of its food ; the proportion or relative prevalence of the different forms of its food, and the fresh and salt water differences ; the condition of the oyster-bed waters, especially as to the amount of oyster foods they contain ; the causes of the variations of the oyster food in oyster-bed waters as affected by season, temperature, and weather; why oysters fatten by immersion in fresh water; and how the colour of food organisms affect the appearance of oysters. "The food of the oyster," says Professor Ryder, "consists entirely of microscopic beings and fragments of organic matter, which are carried by currents from the palpi and gills to the oyster's mouth at the hinge end of the shell. This food when once in the mouth is carried by the action of cilia down the gullet to the stomach, where they undergo digestion and solution. Along with the food much indigestible dirt is taken in, and is cast out with the refuse and waste from the body. This refuse and waste material shows that the oyster subsists largely on diatoms, a low type of moving plants, which swim about in the water, incased in strong boxes. When passed out the living contents have been dissolved out of these diatom cases by the juices of the stomach. Besides diatoms, the spores of algæ, the larvæ of sponges, bryozoa, hydroids, worms, and other molluscs are taken in as food by the oyster at the heads of the small creeks or inlets. Where the water was but little affected by the tides a relative greater development of such minute forms was found."

"In order to examine the food of oysters it is requisite to obtain oysters freshly raked from their beds, and at once to inspect, by the microscope, the undigested contents of the oysters' stomachs. They should be taken from the beds at a three-quarter flood tide; for the greater part of the oyster feeding is then completed. Twenty-four hours after oysters were taken from the bed I found live crustaceans in the stomach. I found also varieties of diatoms and three forms of desmids, which are regarded as existing only in fresh water, although the water from which these oysters were taken was thoroughly salt—sp. gr. 1018—I am inclined to conclude that their presence tended to prove the entrance of fresh water on their beds. These desmids, it is true, had all their fresh-water brilliancy; and the explanation I offer is that the springs and streams of fresh water come up from the bottom at the bed where the oysters thrive, and permits some of the more hardy of these fresh-water forms to live. Among the microscopic forms I noted were rolifers, crustaceans, protozoa, and rhizopods. Living water-fleas and other allied forms were repeatedly taken from oysters which had been twenty-four hours out of water. This indicates that these larger forms are not properly the food of oysters. If they had been they would have been killed and digested in a much shorter time. I think the animal portion of the food of oysters consists rather of larva forms or rhizopods, cyprides, and kindred crustaceans; also the ova and young of small molluscs, and the lower stages of hydroids and bryozoa. But the principal element of oyster food consists of single-celled low-lifed plants, such as desmids—entirely fresh-water forms of vegetable life—and diatoms. The latter constituted at least 80 per cent. of the total amount of oyster food, mostly marine examples. Portions of sea-weed in minute broken fragments are found in the stomachs of oysters, as also are oogonium of some of the oospores and minute zoospores. The proportion of animal to vegetable life found was in 100, diatoms 88, desmids about 1, spores and particles of seaweed 3, crustaceans, vermes and larval forms 8. Many of the diatoms were recognised as fresh-water forms; and their presence points to an important fact in connection with oyster culture. Throughout the Long Island beds there is a greater quantity of fresh water continually present than would naturally be supposed. The presence of desmids, which belong entirely to fresh water, suggests the presence of fresh waterstreams entering the harbour, and flowing several hundred yards without becoming salt. This furnishes a practical hint as to selecting suitable grounds for laying down and cultivating oysters, as well as to the position of building and keeping ponds for their culture. Moreover, it gives us an insight into oyster needs and requirements for a rapid growth and production of oyster food."

"It is a most important point to consider the kind of fresh water and the quantity of it which should be admitted to oyster ponds and beds. As far as possible a moderate supply of ditch or spring water should be continually kept entering such ponds to supply food. I am not advocating brackish water for the cultivation of oysters, but rather the imitation as nearly as possible of the bed water from which the oysters examined were taken. In the case of the Long Island waters we shall have to provide for the entrance of more or less fresh water into them. Along the shore of Long Island a density of 1·017 or 1·018 is sufficient. The most serious defect in our oyster ponds is the neglect to provide for the entrance of sufficient fresh water into them. Its presence in proper quantity increases the amount of diatoms for food; and it also maintains an unvarying density by compensating for the loss caused by evaporation. This alteration of the density of the water is injurious to the propagation of diatoms, and is in a marked degree fatal to young oysters. Warmth and an unvarying temperature, a suitable admittance of fresh and sea water, and the absence of sedimentary accumulations are all necessary for the production and growth of diatoms; and in our waters diatoms, as I have pointed out, compose nine-tenths of the food of the oyster. The probable cause of the failure of Professor Rice's experiments to artificially propagate oysters was the accumulation of sediment on the bottoms of the ponds in which his experiments were tried. So great was the sediment that the greater part of the infusoria in the ponds in which the young oysters lived must have been buried; and what oyster ova escaped suffocation by the sediment were deprived of the food necessary for their existence. His chances of success would have been better had he followed the French culturist's system of ditching or trenching. The sediments would then have settled about the borders, and left the central portions of his ponds clear for the experiment."

Publications consulted in the preparation of this Pamphlet.

Report Royal Commission of Inquiry into the Fisheries of New South Wales, 1880.
Sundry Papers, by Alexander Oliver, Esquire, M.A.
Fish and Fisheries of New South Wales. Reverend J. E. Tenison-Woods.
Mammalia—Recent and Extinct. A. W. Scott, M.A.
Zoology. H. Alleyne Nicholson, M.D., F.G.S., &c., &c.
Dictionary of Dates. Heaton.
Early History of New Zealand. Brett.
Publications, Linnean Society.
Reports of Parliamentary Debates.
Hansard.
Reports of Commissioners of Fisheries, New South Wales.
Report, Royal Commission on Oyster Culture, 1876.
Report, Select Committee of the Legislative Assembly on the Working of the Fisheries Act, 1883.
Report, Select Committee of the Legislative Assembly on the Working of the Fisheries Act, 1889.
Report, Commissioner of Fisheries, Queensland, 1888.

[Four Plates and Maps.]

EXPLANATION OF PLATE 1.

Fig. 1. *Polydora (Leucodore) ciliata*, with ova, from a photomicrograph, highly magnified. Original.
„ 2. Young larvæ of *Polydora* from a photomicrograph, taken shortly after its escape from the ova-sac, highly magnified. Original.
„ 3 & 4. Older stages, from a photomicrograph, highly magnified. Original.
„ 5 to 9. Somewhat more advanced, after Prof. A. Agassiz.
„ 10. Egg-cases of *Polydora*, attached to the side of the membranous tube, x 7 diameters.

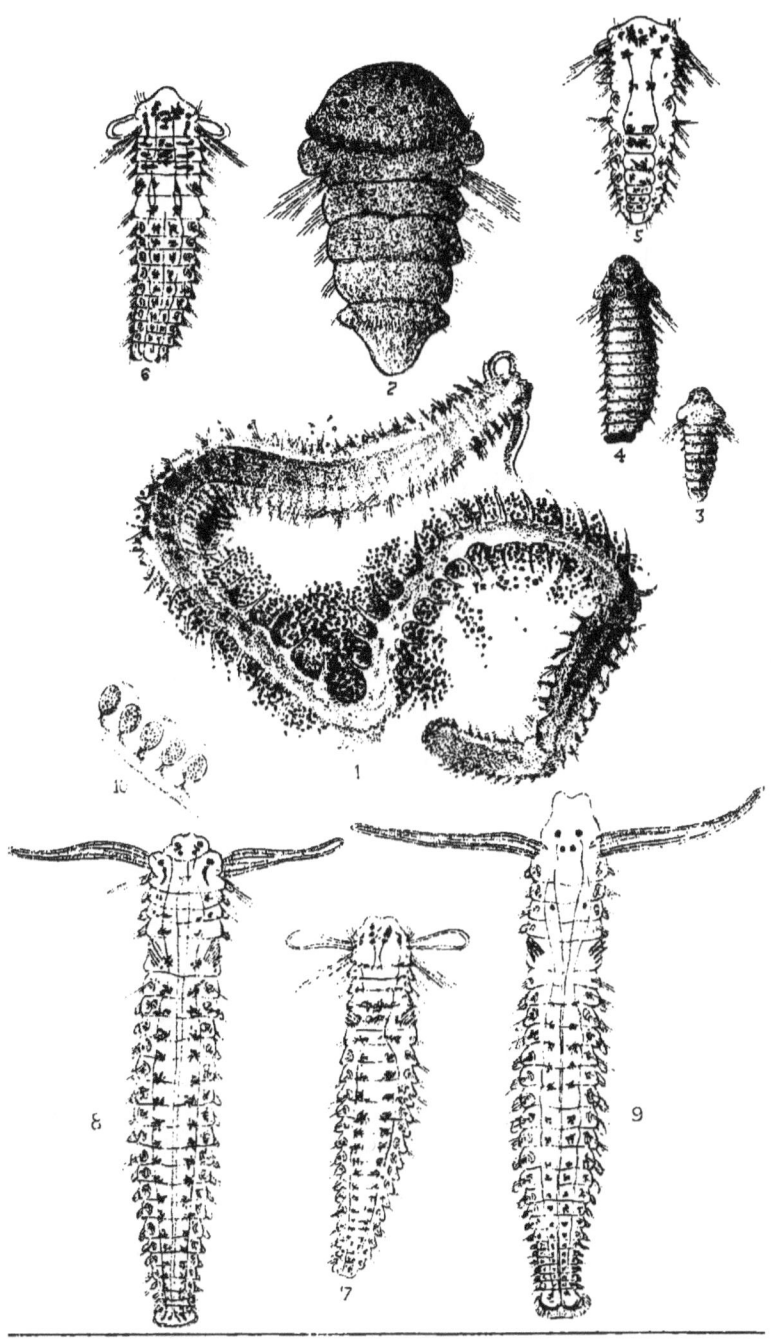

REPRODUCED BY PHOTO-LITHOGRAPHY FROM DRAWINGS BY G. H. BARROW.

EXPLANATION OF PLATE 2.

Fig. 1. Adult worm (*Polydora*) enlarged under a lens.

,, 2. Great hooks of the fifth segment of the body; *a*, as usually seen in the separated and perfect organ under pressure; *b*, more complete as obtained in the living animal or in a favourable spirit preparation x 700 diameters.

,, 3. Spear-tipped bristles accompanying the former x 700 diameters.

,, 4. Hooks of the posterior region of the body; *a*, pressed between two glasses; *b*, seen in front, so as to exhibit both wings, x 700 diameters.

,, 5. Front and side view of two of the bristles of the same species, x 700 diameters.

,, 6. Caudal segment and its cup, x 210 diameters. The whole of the figures and explanations after Prof. W. C. McIntosh.

PLATE 2.

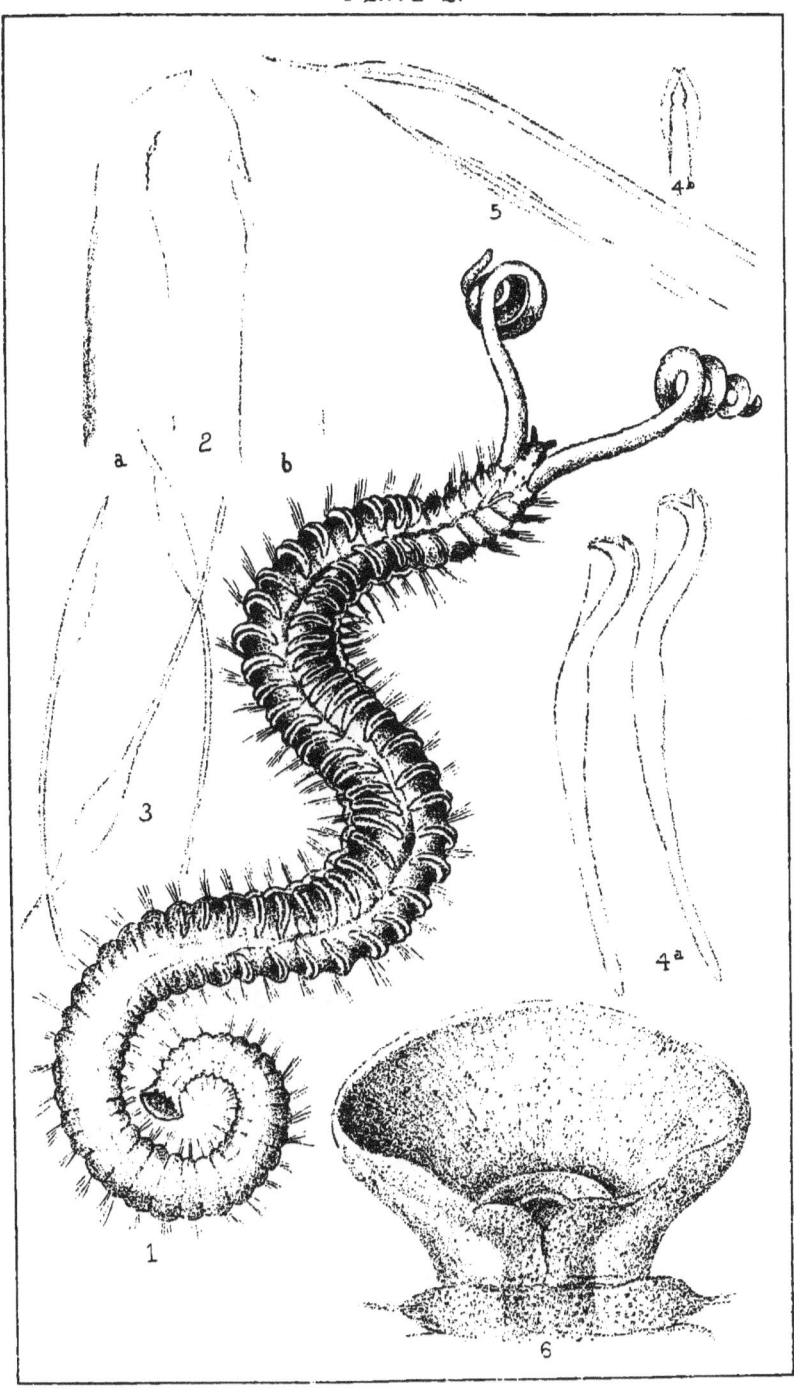

REPRODUCED BY PHOTO-LITHOGRAPHY FROM DRAWINGS BY G. H. BARROW.

EXPLANATION OF PLATE 3.

Fig. 1. Lower (left) valve of *Ostrea cucullata*; (Born) *d*, dorsal edge, *v*, ventral ditto, *a*, anterior margin, *p*, posterior ditto, showing a large blister with the opening of worm tube on the anterior margin.

„ 2. Upper (right) valve exhibiting two blisters; the one with a dotted outline near the ventral edge, is covered by a calcified layer: the other is on the membranous stage.

„ 3. Upper valve showing a larger blister, the work of a single worm (right hand figure). The same with the surface of the blister removed showing the position occupied by the worm (left hand figure).

PLATE B.

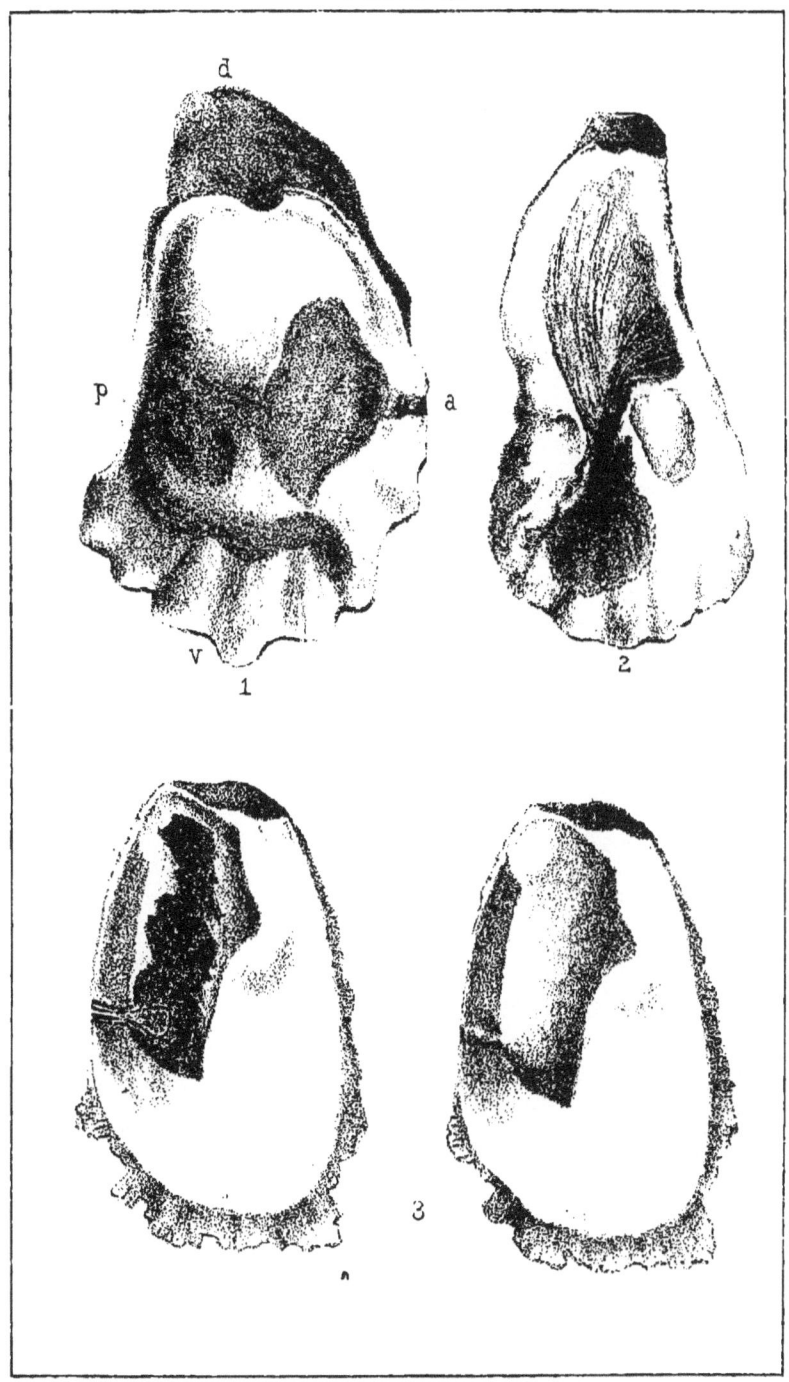

REPRODUCED BY PHOTO-LITHOGRAPHY FROM DRAWINGS BY G. H. BARROW.

EXPLANATION OF PLATE 4.

Fig. 1. Transverse section of lower valve, exhibiting a series of cavities formed by the oyster in its attempts to cover over the various patches of mud collected by the worms. The entrances to some of the cavities may be seen on the right hand side of the figure (the anterior margin).

„ 2. Section of upper valve showing two cavities, with the openings also on the anterior margin.

„ 3. Upper valve showing the extent of the mud patch collected by a single worm, and the surface of the mud covered by a thin uncalcified membrane.

„ 4. Tubes erected by *Polydora* at the aperture of its tunnel. The attenuated tentacles are seen protruding from the mouth of one. Enlarged under a lens, after Prof. McIntosh.

„ 5. Upper valve showing an elevated nodule; near its summit is the tube of the worm projecting at right angles to that of the nodule; the latter is so situated that when the oyster closed its valve there was no communication from without.

„ 6. Edge of an old shell, exhibiting the grooves made by the action of the worms in moving in and out of tubes. The grooves only exist at the margin, and disappear entirely inwards. Slightly enlarged.

„ 7, 8, & 9. Sections of shells showing the openings of the tubes occupied by worms.
Fig. 7 first stage; Fig. 8 second stage; Fig. 9 third stage.
Enlarged three times. See page 8.

„ 10. Portion of a blister showing the inequalities on the inner surface. See page 6.

Plate 4.

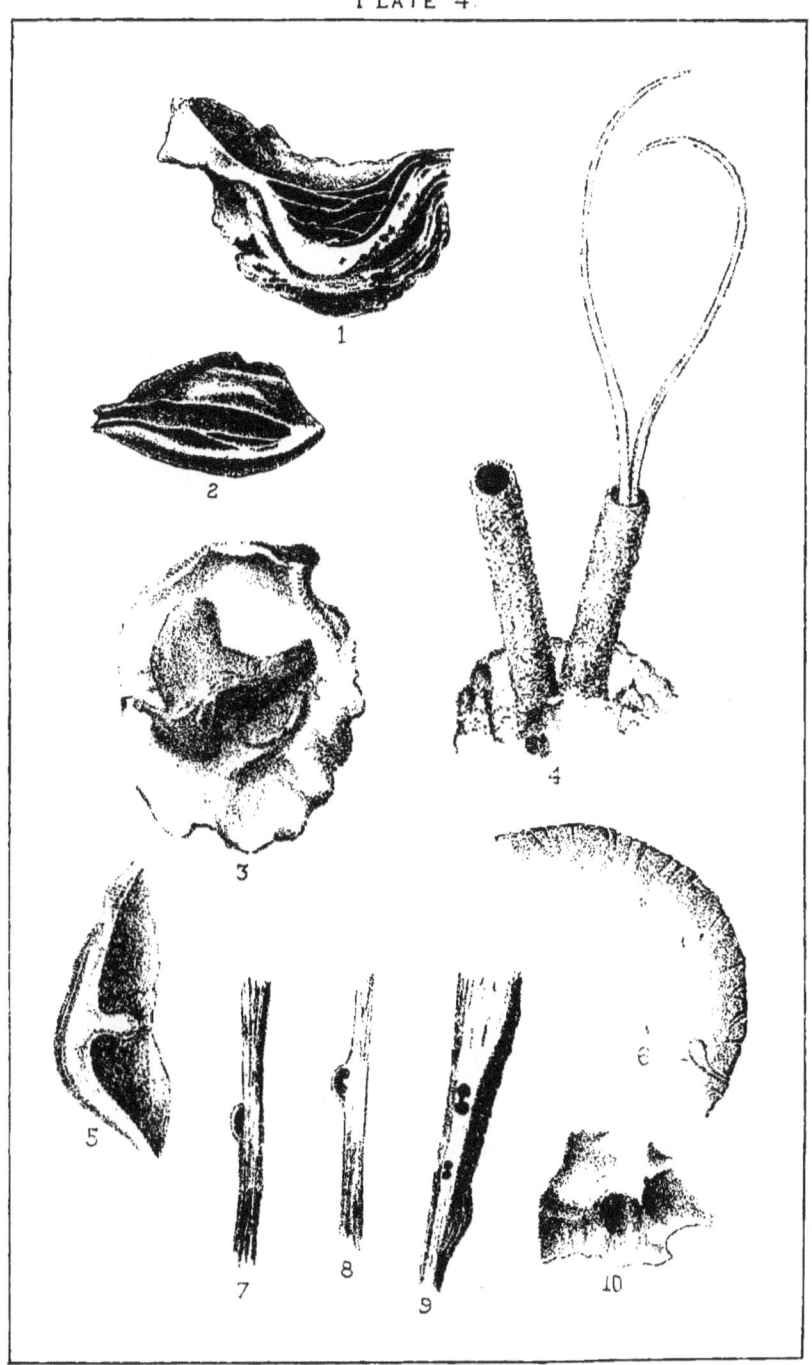

Reproduced by Photo-Lithography from Drawings by G. H. Barrow.

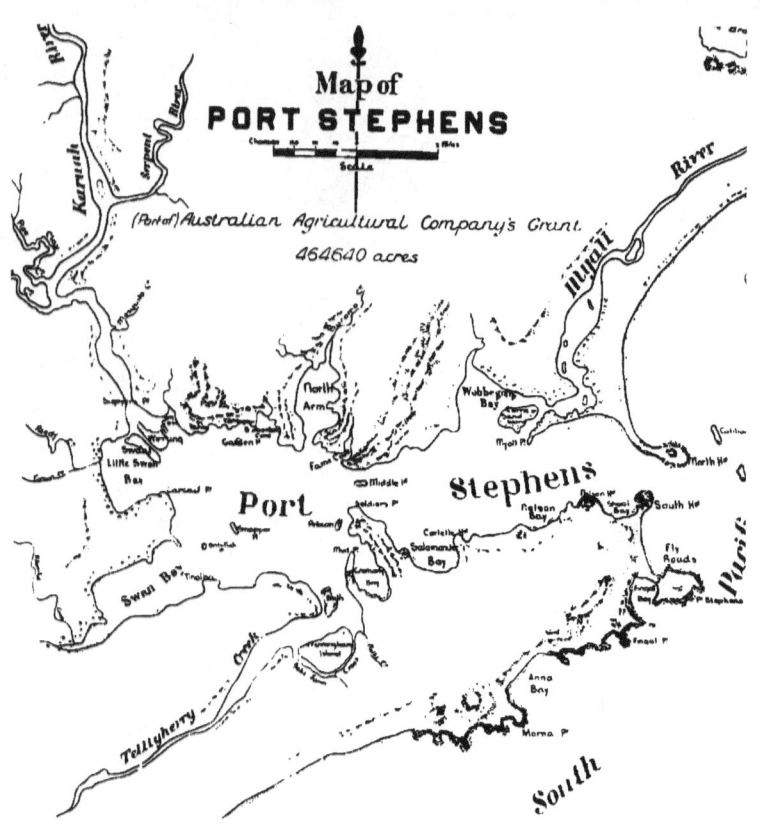

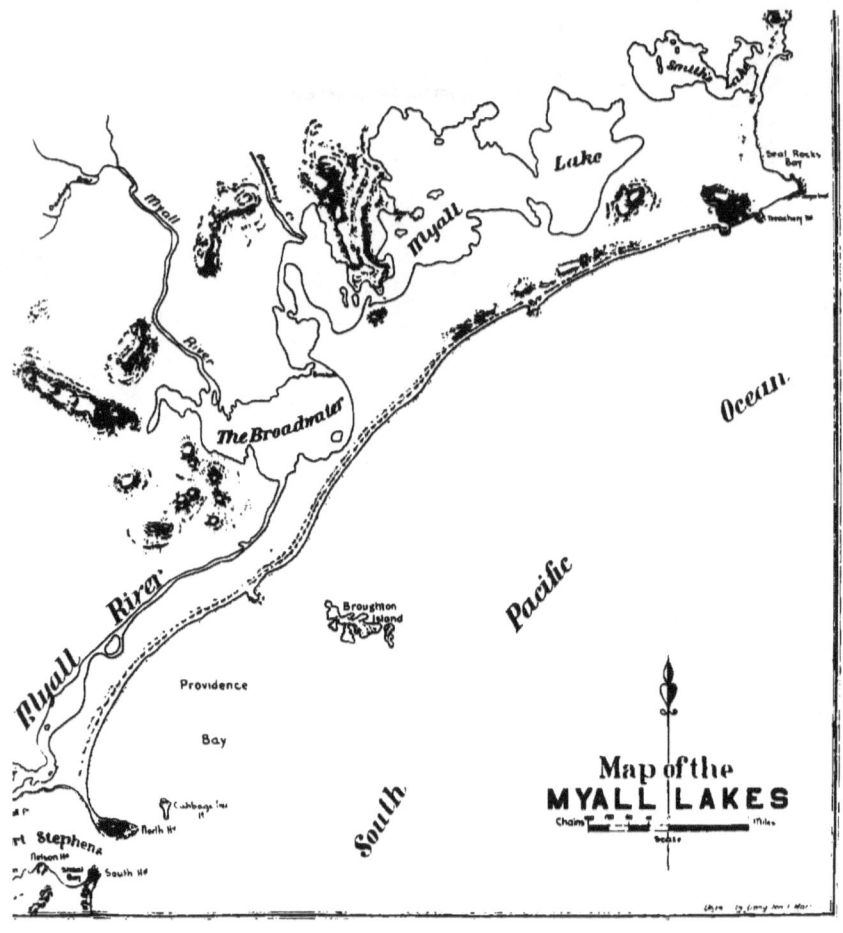

Map of
LAKE MACQUAR

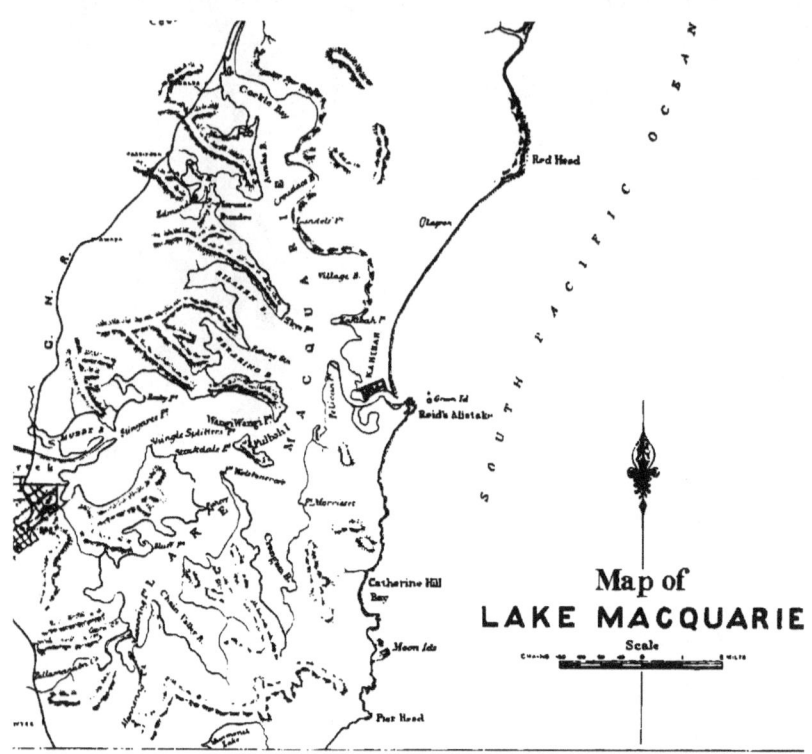

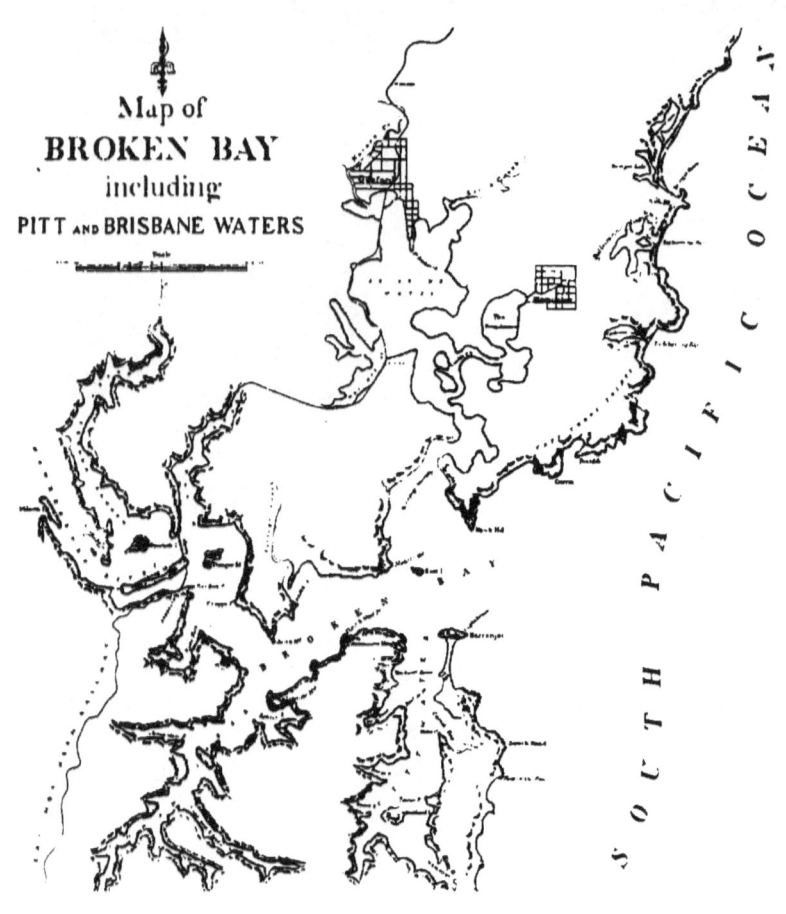

OCEAN

Map of the
ILLAWARRA LAKE
Scale

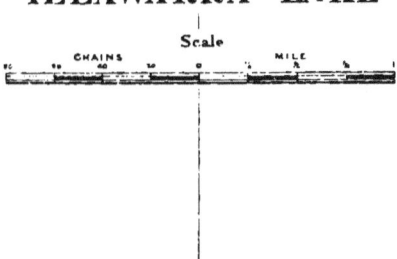

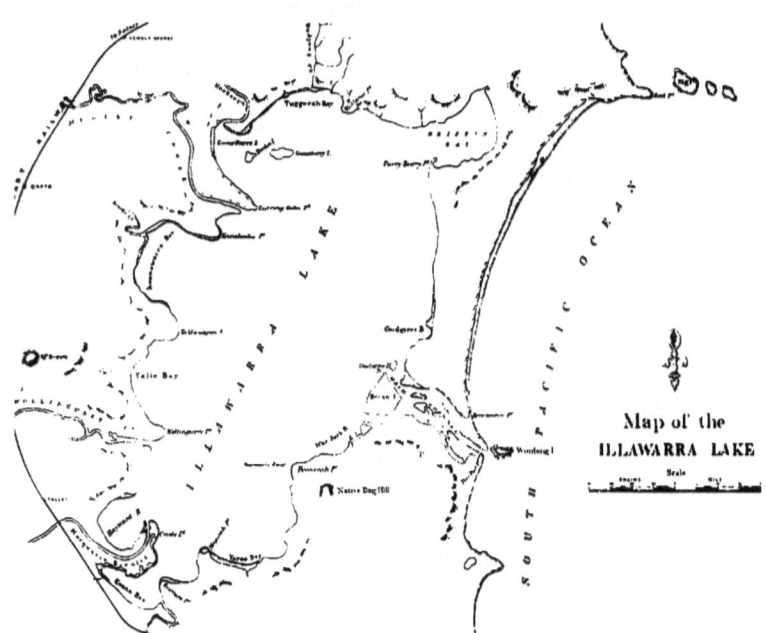

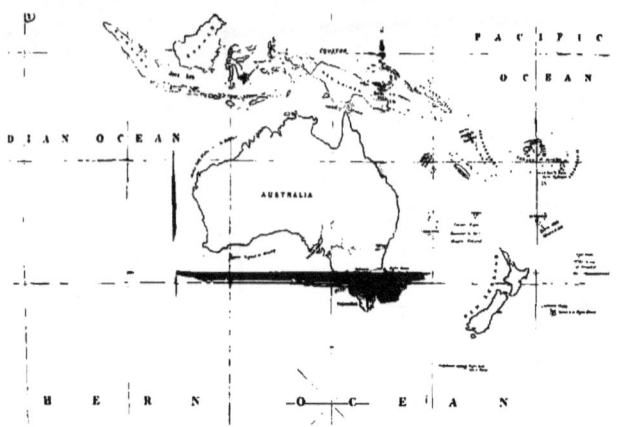

www.ingramcontent.com/pod-product-compliance
Lightning Source LLC
Chambersburg PA
CBHW020827190426
43197CB00037B/722